Selected Books by Merilyn Simonds

NONFICTION

Woman, Watching: Louise de Kiriline Lawrence and the Songbirds of Pimisi Bay (2022)

Gutenberg's Fingerprint: Paper, Pixels and the Lasting Impression of Books (2017)

A New Leaf: Growing with My Garden (2011)

Breakfast at the Exit Café: Travels Through America, co-author Wayne Grady (2010)

The Convict Lover (1996)

FICTION

Refuge (2018)

The Paradise Project (2015)

The Holding (2005)

The Lion in the Room Next Door (1999)

Books by Beth Robinson

My Journey to One Hundred (2023)

Please Write (2015)

Walking with Beth

Conversations with
My 100-Year-Old Friend

Walking with Beth

Merilyn Simonds

RANDOM HOUSE CANADA

PUBLISHED BY RANDOM HOUSE CANADA

 Published in 2025 by Random House Canada, a division of Penguin Random House Canada Limited, Toronto.

Random House Canada, an imprint of Penguin Random House Canada Limited
320 Front Street West, Suite 1400
Toronto, Ontario, M5V 3B6, Canada
penguinrandomhouse.ca

Random House Canada and colophon are registered trademarks of Penguin Random House LLC.

The authorized representative in the EU for product safety and compliance is Penguin Random House Ireland, Morrison Chambers, 32 Nassau Street, Dublin D02 YH68, Ireland. https://eu-contact.penguin.ie

LIBRARY AND ARCHIVES CANADA CATALOGUING IN PUBLICATION

Title: Walking with Beth: conversations with my hundred-year-old friend / Merilyn Simonds.
Names: Simonds, Merilyn, 1949- author
Description: Includes index.
Identifiers: Canadiana (print) 20250131749 | Canadiana (ebook) 20250133679 | ISBN 9781039013346 (hardcover) | ISBN 9781039013353 (EPUB)
Subjects: LCSH: Robinson, Beth, 1920- | LCSH: Simonds, Merilyn, 1949-—Friends and associates. | LCSH: Older people. | LCSH: Aging—Psychological aspects. | LCSH: Old age.
Classification: LCC HQ1061.S56 2025 | DDC 305.26—dc23

Text design: Dylan Browne
Interior images: (embroidery) Choltita, (birds and flowers) isdiyono / both Adobe Stock
Cover image credits: Emilie Simpson, emiliesimpsonshop.com
Typesetting: Erin Cooper

Printed in Canada

2 4 6 8 9 7 5 3

Penguin Random House
RANDOM HOUSE CANADA

For Beth, with love and gratitude

The afternoon of human life must also have a significance of its own, and cannot be merely a pitiful appendage to life's morning.
—Carl Jung, *The Stages of Life* (1930)

"What is it to be immortal?" asked the supplicant.

The muse smiled.

"I am not dead yet."

CONTENTS

One Hundred and Two, Seventy-Two

One Hundred and Three, Seventy-Three

And Counting . . .

Friends

BETH IS ELIZABETH PIERCE ROBINSON, BORN IN KINGSTON, Ontario, on July 22, 1920, a child of the final year of the Spanish flu pandemic. A first child, but not an only child.

Neither of us remembers when we met.

"I feel as though you have always been in my life," Beth says.

I feel that too.

Still, we try to reconstruct. What house was I living in when I was helping Beth with her first book, *Please Write*? I can see myself reading that manuscript in the dormer of my third-floor writing room in our first Kingston house. But I could be making that up.

We try to narrow the frame. No, I never met her husband, who died in 1992. Two years later, she moved into their pied-à-terre in Portsmouth Village, now part of Kingston. In the first year of the millennium, Wayne and I moved out of Kingston to our stone house in the country. When our closest neighbours showed us their stone garden, which Beth had helped conceive, I remember saying, "Yes, I know Beth."

So, sometime between 1994 and the year 2000, Beth and I crossed paths. At a book launch? A reading? Events at the literary festival I founded?

I have a vision of her slim figure in red and black, entirely herself in a way so few people are. I know I felt irresistibly drawn. Maybe

I asked someone who that beautiful woman was. Maybe I introduced myself, although I think I have done that only once, in Mexico, on a beach, when I approached an older woman in a flowing caftan, an American I had seen walking the sand every morning, a woman who had that intelligent self-possession, that instinct for beauty I sense in Beth. The sun had scarcely risen when I stopped the woman and she pressed my hand between both of hers, saying, "I've felt drawn to you, too."

Beth and I agree: It doesn't matter when we met. All that matters is that somehow, somewhere, our lives intersected. And we said to ourselves, *I want that woman as my friend.*

By the time we entered each other's orbit, Beth had raised a family in Toronto, worked in Montreal as a professor of art therapy, and retired to Lower Beverley Lake in eastern Ontario, where she had summered since she was a child, and where she and her husband built a house. After her husband died, she moved full circle back to her birthplace of Kingston. I had just moved there from North Bay, leaving behind the shambles of a marriage, finding new love and a second marriage in this city on Lake Ontario.

For years, Beth and I chanced upon each other in the rousing literary community that made this small eastern Ontario city seem to me like a miniature version of Paris in the twenties. Now, a second pandemic has swept us all into solitude.

Since I was a very young child, words have been my way into life and its mysteries. My machete. My compass. My eyes. But now that I have reached my biblical threescore and ten, I find few books to guide me through this new territory. Those that exist are full of remonstrances—do this! do that! and you will live forever—or they are litanies of complaint. I feel trapped in the grimmest of fairy tales, ogres of pain and decrepitude crouching over every path through these dark woods where my life will surely end.

Louise Glück, the American poet who won the 2020 Nobel Prize in Literature, once said in a *Paris Review* interview: “Anyone who writes is a seeker. You look at a blank page and you’re seeking. That role is assigned to us and never removed.”

I used to look for love and happiness, understanding and security. What am I looking for now?

One Hundred and One

Seventy-One

The Proposal

IN THE SPRING OF 2020, MY HUSBAND WAYNE AND I RUSHED back from our annual wintering grounds in the sunny mountains of central Mexico on what felt like the last flight to safety. We returned to a Kingston mired in the slushy interstice between winter and spring. Pandemic rules locked us down: Isolate at home, see as few people as possible, wear a mask, don't touch, don't hug, don't share a cup, wash your hands vigorously after each and every encounter. We did as we were told; people were dying all around us at an alarming rate, most of them our age and older.

A year later, in March—so lamblike that the streets were suddenly clear of snow—I had just finished writing a biography of Louise de Kiriline Lawrence, a remarkable woman I met when I was approaching forty and she was in her nineties. I have always loved older women, their seeming certainty, and I felt an intense sense of loss as I sent that manuscript off to its publisher. The older I get, the harder it becomes to find women who are older than me, but I knew Beth. Through my first winter in Canada in a decade, we became regular email friends, sharing a love of colour and dance that transports us both.

So I don't know her well, but well enough to call her up.

"Would you like to get together?" I ask.

"Covid-19 is still with us," Beth says sensibly. "How about a walk?"

I walk with Beth along the same route she takes every day: down her street to the corner, right down one long block, left for two blocks to a dead end, then halfway back and left past the French public school, right along another block, and right to complete the slightly wonky square back to her house. The properties we pass are large, although the houses are modest, built around the time I was born, when few families were financially secure and everyone was expected to plant a victory garden.

Two soaring maple trees hold the lawn in front of Beth's house, a 1970s split-level bungalow built in what was once the backyard of the house next door. "Those trees are a gift," Beth says. Her writing room looks into their canopy, a hieroglyph of branches against the winter sky, a lush landscape of leaves in summer. One of the trees is wrapped with a wide green ribbon, a vestige of Beth's hundredth birthday last summer, when she refused a party but a troupe of Irish dancers surprised her with a set dance on the grass.

Beth lives alone, which is how she likes it. "For so much of my life I was surrounded by other people with their needs. Now I am free. If I want to go to my dining table and make things for a while, I do. I live for myself."

Halfway along our walk, a thought strikes me and I pause. "There is something I'd like to talk to you about."

She looks at me so intently I feel tongue-tied. Beth knows how to listen—until a few years ago, she was still working as an art therapist with veterans suffering from post-traumatic stress.

"It's a vague notion," I say finally. "I'm seventy-one. I feel I am entering a new stage, although I'm not sure exactly what it is. You're almost a hundred and one; you've been moving through this landscape for thirty years—"

She points a finger over her head and twirls, tinkles an invisible bell in front of my face. "Ah yes, my journey. We'll talk about my journey. I'd like that."

"It might be a book," I say tentatively. "A road map—but not. And not a biography, definitely not that. More like this present moment—what the view is like from here, from where I am, looking forward, from where you are—"

She nods. "I'm at the stage where I'm most interested in looking back."

"But not just that."

"No, not just that."

We play with the idea in the sunshine of this early spring day, tossing it back and forth until it has some kind of shape. We don't give in to the temptation of tea together. Beth has had her first Covid-19 vaccination, but I haven't. Even with masks, which we wear as we walk, we decide an indoor visit is not worth the risk. And so we part, promising to walk again next week. In the meantime, we'll each make a list of what we'd like to talk about.

I drive away from Beth's house, charged with possibility. We will talk—about everything under the sun.

Old Ladies

THE THREE WOMEN LEAN INTO EACH OTHER IN THE PHOTOGRAPH, laughing. They are old and they're dressed funny, like toddlers, wearing whatever strikes their fancy. Mismatched patterns. Silly hats. Baggy pants. Florid tops. They are standing on the deck of the SS *Rio Tunuyán* as it steams south through the Atlantic from New York City to Rio de Janeiro in the fall of 1956.

They might as well have been passengers on the ship that Jan Morris called *Geriatrica* in an article she wrote for *The Paris Review* in the spring of 2021. The passenger list tilted heavily towards the senior: The first on-board educational lecture was "Facing Up to Rheumatism," although "Facing Up to Decay," notes Morris, would have been more appropriate. "The passengers were divided between those who faced up to the challenge cockily, marching around the promenade deck in obligatory exercise, dressing formidably for dinner, downing G&Ts by the pool. The other half of us preferred resignation, sitting in twos and threes, sipping fruit drinks through flexible straws, playing bridge, adjusting our shawls."

Morris called the two camps Defiance and Resignation, although she came to see that the denizens of both were alike in toughness and resolution, in energetic enthusiasm for whatever was to come next, all of them determined to make the most of everything. By the end of the cruise, she had renamed the ship and all those who sailed in her *Indomitable*.

I was seven when I met the three lovely, lively crones in the photo, but they weren't my first old ladies. I boarded that ship still in love with Miss Goetz, my grade one teacher in the four-room red-brick schoolhouse I walked to every weekday morning. Miss Goetz must have been about sixty; she retired when I was in grade six, old enough to tap-dance at her retirement party. I remember her from the ground up: thick-heeled lace-up black shoes, tweed pencil skirt that stopped mid-calf, a frilly blouse, its hint of flair held in check under a cardigan—cashmere, I like to think, although it was probably hand-knit from some stiff wool. I can't conjure her face or her hair, but I will never forget her voice: stern and cool in the classroom as she insisted a girl in grade two clean up her own vomit, yet strangely softened in the living room of her house by the river on a back street of our village in southwestern Ontario.

I don't know why I went there that first time. Maybe I was delivering something from my mother, who was always sending baking here and there in the village. Maybe Miss Goetz heard I was moving to Brazil and invited me over. Her house was nothing at all like the houses of my friends, with their jumble of parents and children. Her rooms were filled with mementoes from her travels—colourful embroidered cushions, painted candy dishes, candle holders fitted with candles that were lit at any time of day, not just on special occasions. Everything had been chosen and placed by her hand, no other, which gave the rooms, I think now, a singular scent, an unmuddied tone. At the time, I didn't know anyone who had been farther than Toronto, where my grandparents lived, an hour's drive away. But Miss Goetz had travelled to Greece, France, Egypt—names that felt delicious in my mouth. I'd sit drinking tea heavily laced with milk and sugar while she told me about those foreign places, speaking to me like a friend.

Even before Miss Goetz, old ladies were a fixture in my life. When I was five, I contracted German measles just as my mother was about to deliver my baby sister. I was hustled off to my grandmother's house a few blocks away, where I lived for most of the summer as the measles recurred again and again. Miss Calder lived next door to my grandmother in a tiny house at the end of a long path through a tall garden. She was small—a sweet china doll of a woman in her nineties, more my size than any adult. We sat and talked, I don't remember about what, but I grabbed every chance to go over for a visit. I took her little bouquets of phlox from my grandmother's garden and fresh eggs I gathered from my grandfather's chicken coop behind the barn, which sat like a bit of farmyard behind my grandparents' red-brick house. If Miss Calder was otherwise engaged, I'd cross the street to Mrs. Baxter's, who, years later when I married, gave me a teapot with a teacup and sugar bowl all stacked into one, a wedding present my grandmother had given to her fifty years before. A gift I will pass on to a granddaughter.

There were a lot of old ladies in our village, women tucked in small, neat houses, living their independent lives, teaching piano, pruning their roses, baking for school sales, women who could be relied on to donate to the Cancer Society or buy boxes of Girl Guide cookies from the troop of us who went door to door.

I wonder now why I found those older women so appealing. Someone to do for, to make me feel needed? I don't think so. These women—Ellen Stafford, who chose her own name in mid-life, taking it from the British shire where she lived, and who published her first novel the year she turned eighty; Louise in her log cabin on Pimisi Bay, sipping strong coffee, smoking unfiltered cigarettes, getting up before dawn to make her daily bird count, well into her nineties; Erna, who gave birth to her first son in a German barn as she fled the invading Russians—these women didn't need anything from me. What did I need from them?

"They listened," Beth says when I tell her about my lifelong attraction to older women. "Intently."

"I guess they did, but what I remember most is the way they talked to me. Not like other adults, telling me what to do, how to do it. Just conversation. Like what we're doing now."

All of them—from Miss Calder to Beth—lived alone. Some had been married, but when I met them, it was their solitude I admired. Maybe that was because I was the third of four daughters, the mother of two sons, stepmother to two daughters. In my entire life, I have lived alone for only four months: half of one percent of my bygone days. The rest of the time I've lived in overpopulated chaos. The houses of these women were oases of tranquility, a place of cultured, stimulating calm, something I couldn't seem to fashion for myself. They were proof not only that a woman could live on her own but that she could live well. Their resilience drew me. Their forthrightness. They weren't unkind—they had lived too long for that—but they weren't treacly either. They meant what they said. They'd had time to figure out what they believed. Time, too, to open their minds and hearts, to think again. I could rely on them to tell the truth.

"They showed you strength," Beth says. "Consistency."

Now I am the old lady. I dress funny. Today, a long burgundy skirt with sequins and inset lace, a misshapen grey cashmere sweater, sensible zip-up shoes, striped compression stockings, and a vest made from bright scraps of brocade and signed on the inside by the artist, which I bought at the Bodega de Sorpresa in Mexico for a peso-song. Many of the clothes in my closet come from the Surprise Shop, where gringos deposit their barely worn outfits to make room in their suitcases for souvenirs.

Still, I am not so old that I can't find a woman older than I am. Beth is my old lady now. My last guide into the future.

We Begin

I CHOOSE A VIVID TURQUOISE NOTEBOOK AND A FUCHSIA PEN for this project. The colour of my notebook changes from project to project, but the brand remains the same: Blueline MiracleBind, with hard covers, a spiral binding, and pages that can be removed and reinserted somewhere else. I rarely shift the pages around, but I love that I can. On top of my office cupboard, the spines line up in a capricious colour chart, the ideas that became books dominating those that were stillborn.

I show my turquoise notebook to Beth the next time we meet and she shows me hers, a muted hand-stitched gathering of fine-toothed paper between covers that ripple with the stylized waves of the Japanese artist Hokusai. She has pasted my first email into the opening spread, the one in which I laid out what I thought we might talk about during this conversation that could extend for years. She has printed her list on the next page in fine block letters.

Beth's book won't lie flat. And it's small. When I tell her I have ordered two more turquoise notebooks, she asks me to order one for her too.

"Black, turquoise, or purple?"

"It doesn't matter," she says.

I don't believe her. Colour always matters to Beth.

That evening, I fill out an order online. Turquoise for me. Purple for Beth.

Decrepitas

BETH'S MORNINGS BEGIN WITH EXERCISE. WHEN SHE TOLD ME some years ago that she started each day by standing for fifteen minutes against a wall—head, shoulders, buttocks, heels tight to the plaster—I made that my practice too.

"I don't do that anymore," she says as we walk briskly past the French elementary school spilling its bilingual children. "Now I do stretches. And I am always aware of my posture. I correct it a dozen times a day. I don't want to end up like this." She bends low, her back humped, a perfect parody of the white-bearded figure hunched over a cane who trails at the end of the Seven Ages of Man.

I remember seeing a representation of the seven ages in a marble floor mosaic in the cathedral at the centre of Siena, Italy. The series of white figures were set in connecting black octagons: *Infantia*, a child at play; *Pueritis*, a young boy in short cloak and cap, strolling through lush fields; the season of youth—*Adolescentia* and *Iuventus*—spread between flowers and birds; manhood, *Virilitas*, as a studious citizen with an open book, followed by *Senectus*, bearded, in a garden; and in the diamond at the centre, *Decrepitas*, moving across a barren landscape towards an open grave.

Aristotle was the first to make a scientific study of human life. He wrote two treatises, *On Youth, Old Age, Life and Death* and *On Length and Shortness of Life*, in which he presents a biological—and fairly disheartening—picture of aging, which he characterizes as "failing."

The ancient Greeks were especially fond of divvying up a life. The earliest, Solon, sliced life into ten stages of seven years each. An infant until seven, a child until fourteen; a "beard of changing colours" until twenty-one; full manly strength by twenty-eight; a wife and prosperity until thirty-five; a mind no longer pleased by trivial matters until forty-two; during stages seven and eight, from forty-two to fifty-six, a man's understanding and speech are at their best; at sixty-three, he still has some powers, but is "in eloquence and wisdom no longer capable of great effort." In the last stage, approaching seventy, "let him who shall attain the tenth septenary look for a not untimely death."

So this is how the Greeks and the bards see both Beth and me: sitting on our tombs, waiting for certain death. At best, shuffling along, bent over our canes, failing, failing as we move past seventy.

Yet here is Beth at a hundred and one walking erect beside me, sans cane, sans hunch. Her step is firm, not a hint of elderly shuffle. She is talking as she walks, not drivel or gossip or meandering reminiscences, but the thoughtful explorations of a woman who has lived a century.

"We are all expected to go through the same stages," Beth says. "But we don't."

The poet Lucy Grealy, in her correspondence with the novelist and memoirist Ann Patchett, mulled over her evolving self. She was in her twenties, so she considered only two selves: then and now. I'm a half-century older than Lucy was at the time and I can identify at least eight versions of me: my child self, before age seven; my Brazil self; my teenage self; my writer self; my married self; my mother self; my daughter-of-an-aging-mother self; my own aging self.

"I am at a total loss to describe HOW I am different," Lucy wrote to Ann,

> how what I know *now* differs from what I knew *then*. This is a language problem: the disparity between the two selves, between the two sets of truths, is very real and clear to me, yet my ability to control this knowledge in any sort of narrative or verbal way veers off constantly. Like the dreams where you suddenly realize you don't speak the language.

Like Lucy, I have trouble articulating exactly how I am different now from those other versions of me. I used to think that truth was eternal, that once I grasped a truth, it would be mine, like another eye through which to view the world. But there are so many truths, I've realized, that I would need the eyes of an ant, with hundreds of seeing parts, to observe them all. Some truths—the necessity of love, the obligation of kindness—have stayed with me through all my metamorphoses; others have dissolved like teeth in Coca-Cola.

What doesn't kill you makes you stronger. Love conquers all. The world just keeps getting better. Nothing lasts forever. These truths of adolescence are not my truths now. In each of the stages I've moved through, some moment has lifted me out of myself and returned me, changed, to my life. A boy peeing on my shoes when I was eight. When I was fifteen, the death of a child I had babysat for years. The death of a hitchhiker I never met, when I was twenty. My betrayal of a friend when I was thirty. A friend's betrayal of me when I was forty. The loving arms of a choir when I was fifty. The generosity of a city when I was sixty. The astonishing, reliable, no-strings-attached, ongoing devotion of my husband, Wayne.

Some things do last forever. Some lives do not fail at seventy—or a hundred.

Beth slices through the tough skin of history and its fleshy assumptions to lay bare the truth at our core. "Your life is your very own," she says. "No one has a life exactly like yours."

The Sage and the Scribe

BETH AND I ARE READING MAY SARTON'S *ENDGAME: A JOURNEY of the Seventy-Ninth Year.* We've copied quotes into our notebooks that we read to each other as we walk.

Beth: "Old age is a journey into a foreign country so that one is constantly being astonished by what is possible, by what is different from anything that has gone before."

Me: "The trouble for me is that I often loved people much older and wiser than I. So I'm left now in the lurch, being, trying to be, the old wise one and feeling like a great goose."

Beth: "In my normal life I am alone all the time. I work alone. Therefore, when someone comes for tea and it is the only person I see all day, that is precious too, because solitude without society would be meager."

Me: "If you are to grow old well, you must enjoy small comforts."

Beth: "It's not grief that makes me cry but frailty . . . it has been a year of learning how to be dependent."

Beth snaps her notebook shut and stops in the street. "That's not easy for people like us," she says, turning her face away and lifting her black mask a little to breathe in the fresh spring air. "People who have been independent all our lives. Such a leap requires great agility of mind."

Our notebook order has taken forever to arrive. In the meantime, Beth has been making notes in one of the black MiracleBind notebooks I always keep on hand. I have enough of these notebooks in my supply cupboard to last through another thirty years of writing books, and then some.

When I finally deliver Beth's purple notebook, she lifts her pages from the black book and presses them into the purple book, which she hands to me to take home. I flip through the pages, taking in her handwriting. She doesn't write; she prints in swift block letters. My own penmanship shifts with my mood, from a perfectly slanted grade three cursive to the upright, bulbous letters I adopted from my British pen pal in high school. Through my years as a journalist, my words grew big and sloppy. Now my hand shifts between a reincarnated Palmer and all-but-printed vertical text. Whatever the shape of the letters, my words always hug the left-hand margin, which, according to the graphology text I consult, means I tend to live in the past and have a hard time letting go.

Writing in all caps—Beth's style—means she is bold. She knows what she wants.

I slip Beth's notebook and mine into my satchel. Without discussion, our roles, it seems, have been decided. Beth takes the long view: She is the observer, the sage. I am the scribe, the archivist, the guardian of our words.

Uncertainties

I ARRIVE TOO EARLY, SO I PULL TO THE CURB, OUT OF SIGHT OF Beth's house, and wait.

A little girl comes to the end of her driveway and stares at me without compunction. An older couple out walking along my side of the road head straight for me, veering at the last minute, almost smacking into my side mirror, an odd game of chicken. I wave and smile to show I'm not a stalker or someone shilling for an unworthy cause. The woman turns sharply and keeps her eye on me in a way I haven't felt since I was seven and walking alone on the back street of our small village.

As I wait, I think about the conversation Beth and I are about to have. We've given up setting topics in advance; we go where the words take us. I will have to listen intently. Her voice is soft, whether by habit or by nature, and recently an extra measure of quietude has crept in, whether from a stiffening of her throat or from some ongoing congestion no one seems to know, but the result is that her voice is stilled now almost to a whisper.

I try to imagine Beth shouting, but it's such a ridiculous picture I laugh out loud. I'm still smiling when I press her doorbell.

The day is warm and all the houses, it seems, have emptied outdoors. As we walk down the road, Beth is greeted like a celebrity.

She waves at small children, pats each yappy, bouncing dog, compliments women on their hyacinths as they straighten to say hello. Everyone is happy to see her.

As a result, our walk takes longer than usual, more than an hour. Back at the house, as if we have arranged this in advance, Beth goes inside and stands at the far end of the entrance hall. I hover near the door, which she has left open a crack. We are both wearing our N95 masks. We aren't taking any chances.

"I'm having trouble with this lockdown," Beth says finally. She's just been to a lung specialist, a long-awaited appointment. For months she's been taking phlegm-reducing supplements, provoking deep coughs with a green plastic device called an Acapella—I know it well, because I use it too when my asthma flares. She has been to a respiratory physiotherapist for breathing exercises, has removed all the feather pillows from her house. She is compliant and diligent, energetic in her search for good health, yet when she asked the lung specialist if any of her efforts would help, he said, "No, not at all."

"That pushed me down." Beth nosedives her hand towards the floor. "Since then, I've had a hard time getting motivated." She casts a baleful glance into the empty living room, the dining room, the kitchen. "And there's just me."

I wish I could take her in my arms. A single friend of mine says that since Covid disallowed massages more than a year ago, she hasn't felt the touch of another person. This virus has made all of us wary of getting sick.

"If we get it," Beth says, wagging her finger at me, "you and I won't stand a winkle of a chance."

She's right, of course. It's the elderly and medically compromised who are dying, although I have a hard time thinking of myself as part of that cadre. “And now it’s going after people my kids’ age,” I say. “And my grandkids’ age. If anything happened to them, I couldn’t bear it.”

Too late, I realize what I have said. Beth has seen two of her three children into their graves, one of them just two years ago.

She goes down a side hall and returns with a framed photograph. In the picture, she’s around forty, I’d guess, holding the hand of her eldest son, Brian, who clutches one of little Gillian’s hands; her second son, Bruce, completes the chain. Beth is wearing blue walking shorts, a tucked-in white shirt, and knee socks. Gillian has on a dress with a ruffled skirt.

Beth’s hand trembles a little as she leans forward awkwardly to retrieve the photo from me. Gillian died in her sleep after returning from Morocco in the spring of 2019. Because of the circumstances, there had to be an autopsy, then further delays before her body was released. In the first flush of Covid, gatherings were banned, so it was a year and a half before Gillian could be laid to rest—months upon months of uncertainty. I can see from Beth’s face that she is still suffering. Grief strips a person raw, leaves them exposed, vulnerable. Fragile.

“They say that this pandemic is like the Second World War, but it is nothing like that at all,” Beth says, her voice sharp. “In the war, we knew what we had to do. It was hard, but there was no uncertainty. It’s the uncertainty now that will drive us mad.”

But I sense there is more to it today. She seems uncharacteristically low, almost frightened.

“Anything that alters my independence is hugely threatening,” she admits when I ask. “I have to consider how I will deal with dependence—because I can see it coming.”

She lays her hand over the photograph, blocking out her younger son and her little girl so that only her elder son and herself are visible. "Brian and I, we're all that's left."

I note the effort she is making to rise above her dark mood.

"Tomorrow is Brian's birthday," she says, almost brightly. "For some years he lived with me. He still lives close by. After you leave, I'll make him a personal card from the art materials on my dining room table—my new Covid-isolation studio."

Age Limits

I USE THE WORD "STILL" A LOT WHEN I TALK ABOUT BETH. Still driving. Still dancing. Still living on her own. "Still" implies that where this particular activity is concerned, Beth has passed her best-before date. That she shouldn't be doing any of these things anymore.

In fact, Beth has long since dropped off most charts. The only exercise I've ever been able to stick to—Miranda Esmonde-White's Essentrics—offers routines geared to every decade of life up to the seventies, which is billed as 70+, as if once a person hits seventy, they reach a plateau that extends into a future that in Beth's case amounts to a third of her life. In her doctor's office, she tells me, there is a list of ages with the tests one can expect at each one. The list stops at eighty-five.

"Obviously, after that, I can expect perfect health!" She chuckles.

When Beth was ninety-eight and still travelling to Ireland every year to walk the green roads for the month of August, she attempted to insert "1920" into the birth year/month/day request at the computer terminal in the Dublin airport.

"The computer would not accept it. I was told to choose the last available year. I did and the computer was happy. Suddenly, I was much younger!"

A Goddess or Two

IT IS MID-APRIL WHEN I NEXT ARRIVE ON BETH'S DOORSTEP and find a note taped over the doorbell: *Please rap, bell on holiday!*

I knock, a light rat-a-tat.

Beth is dressed in muted blue today instead of her usual cheerful reds. Blue jeans and a long blue knitted jersey, its cowl collar held open with a silver brooch. I want to ask her about the brooch's provenance, but we get distracted talking about shoes—instead of her usual neat black leather boots, she is wearing a pair of Keen sneakers with royal-purple laces—and hats. The top shelf of her hall closet is lined with a dozen hats. I think of my friend Leah, who in her books on dressing like a million advises buying quality over quantity, adding a piece or two to your wardrobe every year. But Beth is a hundred; even at Leah's leisurely pace, quality can't help but become quantity.

Today's hat is a black fedora set on Beth's steely hair at a rakish angle. In winter she wears an Irish woollen hat, not a newsboy or a Peaky Blinders cap but a herringbone flapper hat, which suits her simple bob and the delicate features of her face. The fedora is her signal that spring is here.

We walk our usual couple of kilometres around her neighbourhood, revelling in the strengthening sun. We've been talking about religion, a backwash from the Easter just past.

Beth and I both grew up in churchgoing families. Her adolescence and mine, albeit thirty years apart, were both shaped by economic and political crises. Beth came of age in the most desperate years of the Great Depression, when men lined up for blocks for a bowl of soup, when the jobless marched across the country to Ottawa and work camps dotted the countryside, hundreds of young men sent into the wilderness to build roads to nowhere.

I came of age in the sixties. I was fourteen when John F. Kennedy was assassinated; sixteen when Martin Luther King Jr. was killed by a sniper's bullet. Every day another lynching in the American South; children shot in the back by American soldiers in Vietnam; the Red Guard executing musicians and artists in China; the FLQ blowing up mailboxes at home.

Beth's family was financially stable. And no one put a bomb in my family's mailbox or told me to sit at the back of the bus. Even so, both Beth and I grew up feeling the world was a troubled and troubling place.

"I couldn't believe in a punishing God," Beth says now, "or one that would supposedly confer free will, then watch people tear each other apart."

She started questioning the notion of God around the age of seventeen, almost exactly the age that I turned my back on religion.

"With insight, people can reshape their lives, come to know themselves and use that knowledge creatively. We don't need gods and goddesses," she says, then adds with a grin, "Well, maybe a goddess or two."

Neither of us believes in the Christian god or an afterlife, yet we are both drawn to churches. As a child in Campinas, Brazil, I would stop on my way home from school to sit in one of the back pews of Paróquia Nossa Senhora das Dores, staring up at the angels and cherubs painted on the vaulted ceiling, revelling in my solitude.

"It's the ritual," I say. "The tranquility."

"It's the pageantry!" Beth exclaims. "The theatre!"

In the late sixties, as I was leaving the Church, Beth was being drawn back into the fold, not as a believer but as a woman on a revolutionary artistic mission. In 1969, Clifford Elliot, minister of Metropolitan United Church, a neo-Gothic church in downtown Toronto, asked Beth to work with him to update the liturgy.

"I always wanted to see the arts used in the liturgy: poetry instead of Bible readings, abstract silk wall hangings instead of portraits of biblical figures. In Cliff, I found someone who believed as I did in the *vocabulary* of the arts."

Metropolitan United has a park out front and several outbuildings behind, all of them soon filled by Beth with musical, theatrical, literary, and painterly events. The experimental composer and sound ecologist R. Murray Schafer was brought in to establish a theme that all the artists would respond to during a festival they named "dayspring," an archaic word coined to herald the beginning of the day or, more broadly, the beginning of a new order. In 1969, in Beth's hands, dayspring was a clarion call to artistic action.

"We had all these artists who were on the threshold of becoming big," Beth says. I close my eyes and try to visualize what she was conjuring out of thin air. "Theatre in the park, music in the church. In one of the buildings, a darkened room with a sculpture lit in the centre and pillows scattered about where people could sit and contemplate to Murray Schafer's recording of the ocean rippling over stones."

Montreal's Expo 67 had just closed, a world's fair that not only put Canada on the international cultural map but sparked a wave of artistic innovation across the country.

I was eighteen, in my last year of high school, when my grade thirteen class took a field trip to Expo 67. What I remember are the exhausting lineups and the Québécois boys climbing up the fire escape to our room.

But for Beth, who was in her late forties at the time, Expo 67 and dayspring encapsulated deeply significant moments of her life. "Such ingenuity!" she exclaims now. "Everywhere you looked was bedazzling. We came away thinking: We have the capability to do this, if only we have the opportunity.

"The arts contain the element of transcendence," Beth goes on, her face bright with passion. "A state where you are more wholly whole, moved to be more productive, more generous in your ways. People were hungry for that. I steered them towards other ways of feeling comfort—with colour, form, movement, texture. And by bringing the arts into the church, we were putting a stamp of acceptance on the elusive quality of all that the arts have to offer—showing people new possibilities for their own lives."

She laughs, a subversive chuckle. "In all that time, no one ever asked if I believed in God."

I'm curious. Why the Church? Why not put her energies into a community centre? A women's shelter? A school?

She ponders the question. "I think everything I've done has been done with some anticipation of change. And the Church was in need of change. I looked around at the congregation—it was the late sixties and we were all wearing long, gauzy skirts and embroidered tops—and something in the back of my mind said, *There is hope for change here.*"

Beth is expecting a delivery, so we cut our walk short. Back at the house, we set up lawn chairs under her still-leafless maples. The crocuses are already exhausted, but in their place, clusters of bright white starflowers are blooming.

The delivery man arrives and hands Beth a basket of tulips and miniature daffodils. She sways a little as she sets them on the little folding table by her lawn chair.

"You may have noticed I'm a bit wobbly today," she says after the man leaves. "This is the anniversary of my daughter's death."

"Oh, Beth," I say, reaching out to her. "I didn't know."

I knew Gillian had died in spring but not on this precise day. I'd led Beth into a chat about festivals and goddesses. How could I have so misjudged her mood?

"I didn't tell you," she says, closing the subject.

We stand, ready to say our farewells. Meetings and partings have become awkward with Covid, when handshakes and embraces, kisses on the cheek, all carry the threat of contagion and death.

"Turn around," I say gently.

When she does, I put my arms around her waist and lay my cheek against the back of her neck. Her gloved hands search for mine. It is the best we can do, not quite a hug but close enough. We stand like that for a long while.

Possibilities

BETH GREETS ME AT THE DOOR IN RED RUNNING SHOES, JEANS, a cashmere sweater the colour of cherries, and a soft shawl that is a flaming sunset. Her steel-grey hair is pulled back with a dark headband. I'm often struck by her beauty, but today I have to take a moment to catch my breath.

She has been thinking of subtitles for this accumulation of words that may one day coalesce into a book. "From Retirement to Mount Pleasant," she says with a glint in her eye. Mount Pleasant is the Toronto cemetery where my father's family is buried and where a plot awaits Beth's remains.

"What about me? I don't want to be buried. I've told Wayne to just shove me up the chimney."

We both laugh.

"This book is for women," Beth says, turning serious.

I nod in agreement: The female path through the latter stages of life is not the same as that of a man. For one thing, we live longer. In Canada at the moment, the average life expectancy for a little girl born in 2020 is eighty-four years; eighty for a boy.

As a seventy-one-year-old, I have survived what my mother called "the first great culling," which happens to people in their late fifties—one year, nine of our friends died. Beth has survived the second culling, at seventy-five, which took my mother and Wayne's father. The life expectancy charts don't go past ninety, at which point a woman can expect to live another 5.5 years. At a hundred and one, it's anyone's guess how long Beth will carry on, but she has a theory about why she has lived not only this long but in such relatively good health.

"I suffered terribly from migraines in my forties. An American doctor who had a cottage near ours suggested an elimination diet. For a month I ate mostly rice and greens, then slowly I introduced my usual foods. I'd take my pulse before eating a new food, swallow a teaspoon of it, then ten minutes later take my pulse again. Sugars, whole wheat and rye flour, coffee, and meat didn't make it. I cut them out, and almost immediately I felt better."

Since then, Beth has been mostly vegetarian, nourishing herself on vegetables, nuts, and beans, with fruit in limited amounts.

"I've always been able to say no," she says.

"I could use a lesson in that."

She pauses for a moment, adjusting her therapist's hat. "I am a great believer in intuition," she says finally. "I spent much of my therapy time encouraging people to trust their intuition. If someone says, 'Let's go for a walk,' you listen first to your internal response. *No, that's not right for me at this moment*. Or *Yes, let's*. I would encourage them to listen to that intuitive response. The unconscious is a storehouse of our life experiences, and out of that pool of experiences will come suggestions that are useful and appropriate."

I think of my childhood home, my silent, rigid father, my mother walking on eggshells; all four daughters, like so many women, learning to do the same. "But what if all your life experiences have trained you to do what pleases others?"

"You still have to listen to your intuition," Beth says. "Learn to take a breath. Stop. Listen. Then answer."

She looks at me with concern, and I realize she is not talking theory. She is talking to me.

"I worry you will burn yourself out," she says softly. "You can damage your health by giving too much. Doesn't there come a time when a woman can say, *Who am I really?* And she pauses to hear the possibilities—which will come filtering in if she waits. The big thing is to be open, and to listen."

I'm not good at that. I'm not even sure what "that" is. Give me a task and I'll complete it quickly, efficiently, earning my gold stars. But sit and wait for the cosmos to speak? As my mother used to say to me, "You can't sit still for even a minute!"

Imagine

I SPOT BETH FROM ACROSS THE SPRAWLING PARKING LOT ON the edge of Portsmouth Olympic Harbour, or Hatter's Bay, as it was called in the early 1800s, when it was dredged so boats could deliver coal to Kingston Penitentiary, which looms over the sailboats now. The prison was decommissioned in 2014; emptied of prisoners, it's now a historic site where tourists line up to gawk at the cells and dungeons. For me, it will always be occupied by Convict G852, Josie Cleroux, a young thief comforted by the letters a Portsmouth girl hid for him in the quarry where he did hard time. Letters I found in the attic of the house I moved into when I first came to Kingston—which became the heart of my first literary book, *The Convict Lover*.

The sun is shining and Beth is waving at me, her arm high in the air. She looks like a teenager in her apple-green jeans and fitted black puffy jacket, at her neck a scarf as iridescent as a jewel beetle. She has her pert little fedora on her head and a small black leather backpack over her shoulders.

How I love this woman!

We walk a kilometre or two to a bench that overlooks the lake. Beth flops on it dramatically, legs and arms splayed.

"I'm dead!" Her head rolls back and she closes her eyes as if to prove the point.

"No, you're not. I can see you breathing."

"Am I?" Beth sits up. "I guess I am. Oh, well." She lifts her leg easily to straddle the bench so we can speak face to face. "I can't talk to you sideways."

Beth's deck is being sprayed for ants, so we've agreed to meet here, where walking paths rim the shore of Lake Ontario. As we talk, women in pairs pass us, occasionally couples, and once a box-chested runner pushing a jogging stroller with a sleeping toddler inside.

"My children were always present," Beth muses as the man and child pass. She went back to work when all three were in school, but her children remained her priority. "I told my employers I always had to leave by three o'clock because the children got home at three-thirty. I'd have a 'nursery tea' waiting for them."

As a child, when I was sick, my mother would make me what she called "white tea"—a sprinkle of sugar in milk, the cup filled up with hot water—but I'd never heard the term "nursery tea," which, it turns out, is a light meal taken in the afternoon by children. It wasn't the food that was important to Beth.

"What was important were the stories they told about their day."

The sun is dropping, hitting Beth in the eyes.

"Let's switch," I say, getting up, and she slides to the other end of the bench, riding it like a teeter-totter.

I look past Beth to the abandoned Kingston Psychiatric Hospital, where she did an internship as an occupational therapist in the summer of 1941. Originally called the Rockwood Lunatic Asylum, it was built shortly after the penitentiary. Stone houses of correction press in on us from both sides.

But when I glance down, a brilliant blue catches my eye. Small rocks—four of them—have been arranged at the foot of our bench, brightly painted and printed with slogans.

"Kindness rocks," I say, pointing. Anonymous messages of cheer from one stranger to another, intended to lift a person's spirits during this time when we can't gather or hug or even touch anyone outside our bubble.

It gets better.

All we need is love.

Serenity now.

Let it go!

"Let it go—that's the most important," says Beth as we gather our things to leave.

"May Sarton couldn't let anything go," I say. I'm still mulling over the poet's writings about the last stage of her life. For me, she has become the model of how not to be old: complaining, resentful, quick to be wounded, slow to forgive.

"No, she couldn't let go," Beth agrees. "She was obsessed by her own needs."

Beth pauses for so long I wonder if she is feeling unwell. But no, she is working out an antidote to self-obsession.

"We all need solitary time; we all need to take care of ourselves physically and emotionally. And we all need a passion that is our own. How can we navigate a journey that pushes and pulls at us as hard as life does, unless we can imagine?"

Beth's words stay with me as I head for home. Our vehicles idle side by side at the first stoplight. We wave as we turn in opposite directions, but I feel her still beside me, alight with the notion that imagination, more than diet and exercise, is key to surviving the rigours of later life.

"I wonder how one can be encouraged to imagine," she said before we parted. "How can we encourage the imaginative mind?"

I ponder this for days. Surely imagination can't be learned; it just is. Or is it? We say one person is so imaginative and that another has no imagination, but maybe the only difference between them is that one has had the privilege of developing their imagination and in the other, imagination lies dormant, or is repressed by lack of means, racism, sexism, or a culture that rewards only a certain kind of creativity. But how did the imaginative one learn to trust their sense of wonder, to use it as a springboard for the creative leaps that solve problems, shift a life, fill its gaps? Maybe they had curious parents. Perhaps a teacher who, instead of insisting on a recitation of facts, said, *What if?* Or a neighbour who began every sentence with, *I wonder . . .*

Is Beth right, that imagination and creativity are the secrets to surviving, even thriving, through the final decades? Forget control, mastery, the accumulation of wealth. Imagination is the antithesis of all that; it has no structure, no goals.

Imagination free-associates one's self into being.

An Old Man Mad About Drawing

TODAY I BRING *THE AGE OF CREATIVITY* TO OUR WEDNESDAY visit. The book is by Emily Urquhart and details the last years of her father, the distinguished painter Tony Urquhart, who slid into dementia near the end.

Emily describes how, during his working life, Tony kept a cork-board by the dinner table, on which he pinned sketches that he'd stare at during meals. "Tony always worked in series," she recalls,

> experimenting on a repetition of similar images, to keep the work open-ended. He told me, "You don't do just one painting of a horse. You work on ten horses at once—and if you make some kind of discovery on one of them, you can try it on the other nine." But if you just do one and finish it, you've taken the quality out of the idea.

I wonder if that's what Beth and I are doing, following threads, wandering alleys, some of them blind, looking for a single path to understanding these latter years, when revelation comes with travelling all of them.

In her book, Emily explores the relationship between age and creativity. North American youth-obsessed culture tends to associate peak creativity with the twenties, possibly the thirties. But there is also the "swan-song phenomenon," named for the folk tale in which swans sing most beautifully just before they die. According to this theory, artists at the end of their life produce one final transcendent work before their time runs out.

The swan-song notion came from Harvey Lehman, a psychologist who in 1953 published a landmark study of creative life cycles. Lehman analyzed the works of artists in some eighty creative fields and calculated the "maximum average rate of highly superior" production. He declared that the prime age for producing the best oil paintings is 22 to 26; the best lyric poetry, 26 to 31; and the best novels, 40 to 44. The best art is created in youth and early middle age, Lehman declared, and then again just before an artist dies, with one last artistic gasp.

Beth and I raise our eyebrows at each other.

"Henry Moore sculpted *Reclining Figure* at eighty-four," she says. "And Frans Hals produced those masterful group portraits when he was eighty."

"Edna O'Brien published *Little Red Chairs* when she was eighty-five and *Girl* at eighty-eight."

And Tony Urquhart, who died at eighty, painted right to the end, albeit on an invisible canvas with invisible paint, inspired by invisible children playing happily at his feet.

We troll the arts for other examples, which are numerous. But Emily argues that the whole swan-song theory is bogus. She quotes studies that associate thinning of the frontal cortex, which happens naturally as we age, with lowered inhibitions, "enabling creative behaviour and thought." Writers, especially, get better as they get older. Roger Angell, Wayne's favourite baseball writer, wrote his last piece for *The New Yorker* the year before he died at a hundred and one. He also wrote wonderfully about the challenges of aging, saying at ninety-three that old age sometimes felt like a "blankness, invisibility." He would say something at a dinner party only to hear silence in return. "Hello? Didn't I just say something? Have I left the room?"

Beth and I revel in Emily's research. What older person doesn't cheer to know that the average vocabulary of a retired adult is 25 percent larger than that of a college student? That older people apparently have something called "crystallized intelligence"—deep wells of knowledge gathered over a lifetime—that more than makes up for the white-hot smarts of youth.

In *The Age of Creativity*, Emily quotes Hokusai, the Japanese artist best known for his woodblock print series *Thirty-Six Views of Mount Fuji*, which includes the iconic *Great Wave Off Kanagawa*, the image on the front of Beth's initial notebook. Shortly before Hokusai died in 1849 at the age of eighty-nine, he stopped calling himself Hokusai and instead signed his prints "The Old Man Mad About Drawing."

"I have drawn things since I was six," he wrote. "All that I made before the age of 65 is not worth counting. At 73, I began to understand the true construction of animals, plants, trees, birds, fishes, and insects. At 90, I will enter into the secret of things. At 110, everything—every dot, every dash—will live."

I am stopped short by Hokusai's assertion. The immodesty of it. If I said such a thing, I'd worry that the gods, having heard my plan, would move heaven and earth to disrupt it.

But what Beth hears from Hokusai is the importance of learning all the way through life. Even at the end, he was looking ahead: He had a vision for the next thirty years.

"I do, too," she says quietly.

Amplitude

EVERY MORNING, I SPEND TWENTY MINUTES WITH MIRANDA Esmonde-White—or at least her recorded image—stretching and strengthening the six-hundred-plus muscles in my body. I'm not naturally inclined to exercise. I have come to it late, driven by a horror of developing an old person's saggy-bummed shuffle or that rooster posture favoured by formerly active, heavy-bellied men: elbows pulled back, neck forward, knees permanently bent.

Thanks to Miranda and her Essentrics workouts, and years of prodding from my physiotherapist sister, my posture is pretty good, yet when I walk with Beth, I find myself pulling on that invisible string attached to the top of my skull, straightening just a little more. Beth is a posture queen.

"I remember seeing a dancer at the Toronto Dance Theatre, stretching out her arm on stage," Beth recalls. "You wouldn't believe how far that arm could reach. It was breathtaking."

Miranda Esmonde-White is teaching me to extend my reach. She was once a dancer with the National Ballet of Canada and developed her exercise program in reaction to the unnatural demands made on a body by dancing and by the fitness industry. Instead, she bases her routines on how a human body was designed to move. So I trust her when she tells me that instead of straining to reach, I must relax my arm in its socket, then stretch. Miraculously, my reach grows by at least an inch. I relax the joint some more and stretch again. Amazing! If I needed to, I could scoop up Wayne's dessert from across the table.

Twyla Tharp, the choreographer and dancer, in her book *Keep It Moving: Lessons for the Rest of Your Life*, urges her readers to "take up space." Dancers are taught to move so that every gesture is not only precise and elegant but BIG. Dancers call it "amplitude"—the opening of a move in every direction to its full expanse. Think the same way in everyday movements, Tharp advises. Stride, don't mince. Extend your arm fully to shake a hand or embrace a friend. Instead of retreating into yourself with age, occupy more space.

Beth may be petite, but she definitely occupies space. She moves like the dancer she is.

"I've been dancing all my life," she says. When she was seven, her mother enrolled her in the Myra Cruikshank Studio for dance and elocution, where she learned not only to listen acutely to words and speak distinctly, but also to plié, tendu, and arabesque. When she was nine, she graduated to the Royal Conservatory of Music. In the early 1930s she studied ballet with Bettina Byers, a professional ballerina who, when asked why she wanted to dance, replied, "I was born that way." The same could be said of Beth.

After she married, Beth and her husband, Jack, took up square dancing, which was all the rage in the 1950s and '60s. My parents square-danced too, on the marble floor of our Brazilian garage. And when Jack died, Beth took up Irish set dancing, a form of folk dancing based on court quadrilles, where four or eight dancers move without a caller to traditional Irish "sets" such as Garden of the Daisies and King of the Fairies.

"In Irish dancing, you have to be so aware of your posture," Beth says.

I nod as if I know. I took dance lessons too, in Brazil, making my way every week to a room full of nine-year-old girls. None of my sisters danced, but I loved it. At the end of each season we'd put on extravagant recitals at the opulent São Carlo Theatre, recitals that made me feel like a real dancer: the magnificent giant FIFA cup we danced around after Brazil won the world soccer championship in 1958; the beautiful, slender ballerina who joined us for one last Hungarian Dance, her arms and legs impossibly long, our troupe of gangly neophytes tottering in our first toe shoes, feeling more elegant than we could ever hope to be.

As a teenager, I painted acrylic paisleys on a miniskirt that I sewed from sandpaper cloth my father brought home from his factory, and, with a friend, put on my white go-go boots and danced on a raised platform to the music of a local band. I danced on tables at bars. Later, when Mexico became my winter home—technically for the dry desert air that soothed my asthmatic lungs, but really for the colour and the music—I watched the people at the Sunday *baile*, dancing around the bandstand in the middle of the park that holds the centre of town. When the music stopped, I went up to the best dancer in the crowd, a slim older man wearing soft white shoes and a white straw hat who had danced with many women, each one becoming Ginger Rogers in his arms. I asked him in my halting Spanish if he could teach me to dance the cumbia. "*Si, señora*," he said, explaining that he was a mechanic by day but at night he worked as an instructor at the Arthur Murray Dance Studio. For the rest of the winter, he came to my house after work on Friday afternoons and we danced the cumbia, a partnered dance with a few basic moves and endless variations that one partner communicates to the other through a slight pressure on the hand or spine, although it is the dancers' gaze that says the most.

"*Nunca dejes de mirarme a los ojos*," he'd say. Never stop looking in my eyes.

Beth and I both love to dance, but her affection is of a different order than mine. In 1968, during the years she was spending her summers at Lower Beverley Lake, one of her Kingston friends asked her to help with a summer school of the arts she was creating for local children. Among the artists Beth met there was David Earle, who had studied with Martha Graham. He told Beth that he and some friends were forming a modern dance company called the Toronto Dance Theatre. She immediately volunteered and eventually became chair of the TDT School of Dance. When David moved to the Guelph area and formed Dance Theatre David Earle, Beth joined his board of directors. "And there I remain!"

After our walk, Beth sends me a YouTube talk on Françoise Sullivan, a dancer of her generation, now on the cusp of a hundred. One of her performances, *Danse dans la neige*, has become iconic in Canadian cultural history—a profoundly moving piece danced outdoors to the sound of her own footsteps crunching the crusted snow. The only audience was the landscape, the painter Jean-Paul Riopelle, who documented the performance on film, and Maurice Perron, who photographed it.

For several weeks, dance occupies our walking talks. We ponder our love of dance—the moving of our bodies and the appreciation of the musical movement of others. Where do such passions come from?

"It's like a family tree, very hard to trace," says Beth. "But my mother's influence was formidable. She loved to dance."

I remember my parents dressing up to go out dancing, my mother in a crinolined aqua dress that Marilyn Monroe might have worn, heels so high she seemed on tiptoe. My father would pull me onto his shoes in my stockinged feet and he'd two-step me around the room. I'd press into his neck, into the scent of wild forests on his skin, happy to be in the arms of a different father altogether from the one who kept us quiet at the dinner table. Their dancing began in Brazil, and so did mine. Brazil, where music laced every day and someone was always dancing in the street.

"I never imagined my passion for dance would last as long as it has," Beth says. "But passions have no life expectancy. We have to have passions—otherwise, our brains will wizen up."

"Our bodies, too," I say.

If this were a musical, we'd pop out of our chairs at exactly the same moment and stag-leap down the street, pirouetting as we go, reaching and rising far beyond our grasp.

Empress of Radical Happiness

BETH IS COMING TO VISIT! I CAN COUNT ON ONE HAND THE friends who have stepped over our threshold in this first year of pandemic isolation. But Beth is vaccinated and so am I. Neither of us is symptomatic, but we test anyway. Negative!

The weather is more like March than the last day of April: rain and cloud and a sharp north wind. I offer to pick Beth up and bring her to our place, but she insists on driving. I meet her at the entrance to the underground garage, where the cement columns are placed perilously close. She gets out and hands me the keys and I move her vehicle into its slender space.

I have set the living room chairs a safe eight feet apart; we both wear masks until we are seated with tea at our elbows. In Beth's honour, I have brought out the porcelain teapot Wayne gave me one Christmas. A long-tailed hummingbird swoops in relief across the belly; the lid is an opening flower. I've set out two teacups: my grandmother's Nippon bowl, porcelain with a gold rim and a hand-painted pink blossom, and my mother's favourite cup, a flaring hexagonal flute that resembles a pale amaryllis, delicately painted with a pointillist English garden.

Beth chooses the flute, as I thought she might.

Our excuse for defying the public health stay-at-home order hangs on the wall. In the depths of our first winter in Canada in more than a decade, my husband and I bought an enormous painting of San Miguel's distant desert hills by Katharine Bruce, a Canadian artist who works in Mexico half the year. I spotted the painting the first time we visited Katharine's house. The image was inspired by the view from her rooftop terrace and by the cactus garden outside her studio. For me, the painting is Mexico.

"The colour!" Beth exclaims the minute she enters the room. "The energy of those lines!" She reaches to touch the filaments of electric blue, white, gold, and hot pink that flash across the canvas like carnival streamers.

"And look at this," I say gently, laying my hands on her shoulders and swivelling her to face the opposite wall.

She gasps.

"Meet the Empress of Radical Happiness," I say.

The oversized huipil created by our San Miguel friend Lena Bartula is part of a series she based on the iconic Meso-American blouse. Huipils are still worn by village women throughout Mexico and Central America. The cloth is typically handwoven and embroidered at the neck and down the front. The one on my wall is a collage of found fabric, scraps of cloth and lace stitched here and there with bright pink-and-turquoise threads and, at the neck, a golden fringe that might once have held back a theatre curtain.

"Our other great extravagance," I say.

"Oh no," Beth protests. "Not an extravagance. I believe this is essential."

We sip our floral tea and nibble on the soft Japanese cotton cake I made in the hope that Beth, with her troubled throat, could swallow the airy concoction of eggs, lemon, yogurt, and a scant spoonful of sugar. We shift our chairs so we can see both the Sierra Madres and the Empress.

"I've always had this 'hand' thing," Beth says. "When I was younger, I set up a loom in my living room. I did pottery, collage, smocked dresses and nighties. There was even a time I wanted to go to England to study embroidery. That never happened, but I did contribute to a huge embroidered piece that's hanging in Toronto City Hall. Embroidery was something I could do as a young mother."

Beth was one of a hundred members of the Toronto Guild of Stitchery who put in the equivalent of more than six years of labour to create a magnificent work of fabric art. It depicts almost a hundred historically significant people and events, the Guild's contribution to Toronto's 150th anniversary celebrations in 1984.

"I look at the Empress and I think, *I should do this*," she says a bit wistfully.

I tell her the Mayan story of how the world got its colour: The gods of the grey world went looking here and there, and when they found a colour, they tossed it into a wooden box. But soon the gods tired of the search, and when they left to have a drink, the colours leapt about and made love until there were so many colours they tumbled out of the box. The gods didn't know what to do with all those colours, so they gathered them up and climbed to the tops of the trees, where they flung them about. The blues stuck to the water and the sky, the yellows drifted up to the sun, the greens landed on the trees and plants, and the browns—the heaviest—fell to the earth. The people were watching open-mouthed, and the red dropped onto their tongues.

The morning after our tea party, Beth sends me an email. She is frugal with her digital correspondence. Emails are rare and often short, but sometimes, like today, her missives are as long and thoughtful as the letters she slides into the postbox.

"What is there about colour that wraps itself around you and lingers long?" she writes. "Today the colours of your new painting and fibre art, and of course your teacups and teapot, linger to walk each step with me. What a feast it is!"

Collage

PAINTINGS COVER EVERY WALL OF BETH'S HOUSE, EYE LEVEL to ceiling. A huge wave rising. Boulders on a shore with clouds like drifts of stone above them. Small gilt-framed villages. A large abstract that could be an oriental robe: rectangles of grey and black and an impossible cerulean relieved by slashes of stark white. Not a still life among them.

I've been in Beth's house before, but the Covid gap makes the place seem new, even though nothing has changed except the dining room table, which is awash in objects.

"Awash" gives the wrong impression. In the centre is a heap of stocking-like shapes with cords dangling from the tops, the thready undoings of some former mobile. Small white stones take up a vaguely rectangular space. On one side, shells that range in size from tiny scallops and periwinkles to the spiralling former homes of hermit crabs and whelks; on the other side, black stones that look like puddles of polished marble. A handful of twigs. A neat stack of Japanese papers in intricate patterns. A few skeins of bright embroidery thread. Thin blocks of wood—some the size of a matchbox, others as big as a deck of playing cards—are stacked, roughly cut from what looks like unfinished shiplap siding. A scattering of pressed dull-red maple leaves. The materials aren't rare or expensive, just bits and bobs she's been gathering on her walks for years and the gleanings that friends have brought her.

"I like how they feel," she says, her finger caressing a length of chartreuse thread.

Centred in front of her chair is a finished "painting" of torn rice paper in soft blues, searching reds.

"The art comes from here," she says, punching herself lightly in the chest. "I don't think or plan, I just move bits of thread and paper and stones around until it feels right."

Beth leads me into the living room and sits in her wooden armchair. Beside her on a small table, dark twigs are silhouetted on a rectangle of bright white paper, a forest in moonlit snow. Nothing is glued in place. The pieces aren't mean to be permanent.

I think of the *alfombras de aserrín*, the sawdust "rugs" that Mexican families press over the cobblestones, working through the night before Christ arrives for Easter, creating brilliant images of the Holy Family, flowers, and crucifixes, all of it obliterated within hours by the feet of singing pilgrims moving down the street behind life-sized wooden statues of Jesus, Mary, and Saint John the Apostle.

When a piece is pleasing, Beth moves the construction—she calls them her collages—from the dining room to this little table by her armchair, where it stays until a new idea, another urge, moves her. Then she sets the collage on the floor, photographs it, and dismantles it, returning the materials to her dining table to become something new.

"It is important that the materials are there on the table, where I can pass and pause and create spontaneously," she says, waving an arm over the sticks and stones and scraps of paper and thread. "I just go to the table and—*whoosh!*—I'm off on a journey."

"Out of yourself? Or deeper in?"

"Oh, deeper. Deeper. I go there and the world moves away."

"I'm not a scavenger by nature," Beth says. "It is a miracle that I came to this thing that is so right for me."

On the day that Covid-19 was declared a pandemic, her friends from the Toronto Dance Theatre, David and his partner, Michael, were visiting. David is twenty years younger than Beth, still teaching dance at eighty-one. After Covid hit, he began choreographing dances in which each dancer recorded themselves individually, remarkable dances of isolation and hope. Every month, David sends out a "Postcard," an email collage of paintings, photographs, poems, song lyrics, musings on a single theme—the Blue Moon of August, Seasons of Change, Love—some of which have been collected as *A Handbook for Ecstatic Survival.* Beth calls these two creative men her pals, a round, loving word that she holds even closer than "friend."

"David has been keeping journals for as long as I've known him. They are a record of his travels, the beginning of every choreography. When he was visiting at that momentous time, he used my printer to print some photographs. He was trimming them for his journal and was about to throw away the thin white trimmings when I said, 'Wait! I can use those!' I took them to the dining room table, and that was the beginning of what is saving me now."

She takes out her iPhone and shows me photograph after photograph of white rectangles on black paper, ascending like crazy staircases, overlapping into the distance like doorways or a jumble of mismatched windows. She has images of more than eighty collages in her phone. My mind searches for meaning, but Beth isn't trying to mirror the world so much as catch its spirit in some new arrangement of the basic elements of shape, colour, texture.

When Monet painted water lilies in his seventies, the blurred brush strokes were dismissed by critics as a symptom of cataracts. He was painting what he saw, they said. Now we understand that he was painting not what he saw, but what he felt. His creative powers weren't diminished with age; his focus had changed.

Beth doesn't cast about for theories as to why she does what she does at her dining room table.

"Beauty sustains me," she says.

Beauty

TODAY ON BETH'S TABLE ARE THREE STACKS OF WOOD SQUARES; on each, a piece of paper the colour of spring peas; on each paper, a white stone that is vaguely heart-shaped, small enough to hide in the palm of the hand.

But what catches my eye is a loose weaving of coloured paper strips that reminds me of one of Lena Bartula's artworks, the one she used on the cover of her book *Whispers in the Thread*—a fabric collage made of dozens of colourful zippers, unzipped to reveal scraps of paper printed with women's words.

Never again.

Mine is not the only truth.

Just listen to me.

Beth's plaited strips carry words too, but before I can decipher them, she calls me to the kitchen to admire a bouquet of white tulips, their stems just beginning to lean into amplitude.

That evening, as I pass by a bowl of shells I keep on the low wall that surrounds our bathtub, I slide out the smallest ones, pink as a baby's fingernails, tiny shells I gathered on the Atlantic shore where Wayne and I spent our honeymoon. I stand there for an endless moment, shifting one shell, then another across the flat white top of the wall, until I pause and think, *This is beauty.*

Demons

BETH'S ANXIETY IS ON THE RISE AGAIN, BUT SHE IS NOT ONE TO leave such feelings to fester.

She tells me about one of her closest friends, a man who believes in rituals. Every day, he sets aside a certain time to confront his demons.

"I decided I had to do that too. I sat down with my yellow pad of paper and a pen and wrote about what the pandemic is doing to me, what it is like to be going through these Covid times without my daughter. I went deeper and deeper. Then I wrote a poem about my daughter and I realized *that* is where the anxiety is coming from."

I lean forward into the heart of her story.

Beth says, "I am afraid to die without my daughter. I always thought she'd be with me at the end."

I think immediately of something I read in Joan Didion's memoir *The Year of Magical Thinking*: that there is simple mourning, filled with sadness, regret, perhaps loneliness, but which doesn't disrupt daily life; then there is the complicated, visceral grief that hits in waves, choking you, plunging you down until you gasp for breath, a grief that can last for years, that comes with the death of someone whose life is intricately interwoven with your own.

Beth called her friend of the rituals, whose background embraces both art history and psychiatry. "I am in trouble," she said to him, "and I know you can help me."

"Hang a lantern out in the garden," he suggested, "and light it at the same time every evening."

Beth takes me out to her back porch, where she has fastened an iron lantern to the corner of the railing. Inside the lantern is a blue-green candle that she has been lighting every evening at dusk. The candle, for her, has become Gillian's presence.

"For all of us, there are times when a ritual that has a connection with your soul, your mind, and your spirit can have a steadying influence." She puts her hand on the lantern. "This is mine."

Secrets in Plain View

I AM HARDLY IN THE DOOR WHEN BETH HANDS ME A GIFT BAG. Inside are some books I loaned her and, laid on top, a thick fold of creamy cloth.

"Would you wear this?" Beth asks, shaking out the cloth and holding it up to me.

"A huipil!" I exclaim. "Yes, of course I will."

"I bought it in Mexico on one of the trips Jack and I took there, in the seventies, I think."

This blouse is as old as my children, but the technique it embodies is ancient. It's been woven on a backstrap loom, a kind of weaving that uses not only a woman's hands but her whole body. I've seen Mexican women weaving this way in the courtyard of the anthropological museum in Mexico City and also in the shade of adobe houses in the villages we've passed through. The warp threads are tied to a tree branch or hooked over a door and secured at the bottom to a wooden stick with a strap that goes around the weaver's hips. As she leans back against the strap, the warp tightens so she can feed the weft threads through.

With my finger, I trace the three narrow woven panels that were sewn together to create this wide strip of cloth that was then folded in half and stitched up the sides to make armholes. In the centre of the fold, a neck hole opens in a V.

I eye the openings. I am an average *norteamericana*, much larger than the average Mexican woman, especially an *Indígena*. Larger than Beth too, who seems slighter every time I see her.

I take off my glasses and ease the huipil over my head. For a moment I worry I'll tear the opening, but I manage to wiggle it over my ears and it fits, just barely. My hands find the armholes. I can hardly breathe, not because the blouse is tight—it's as loose and airy as a huipil is meant to be—but because the sensation of being inside this piece of cloth, wrapped in this boxy shape that women have been weaving and wearing since before the Spaniards arrived in Meso-America five hundred years ago, is overwhelming.

"Wherever did you get this?" I ask, almost in a whisper.

"Tijuana."

I want her to tell me more—the name of the woman who wove the cloth, the name of her village, what the embroidered symbols mean and whether they were worked by the same hand that wove the cloth and sewed the seams—but that's the end of the story for now.

Beth helps me lift the huipil over my head. I hand it back to her, but she shakes her head.

"It's yours."

Lena Bartula has been studying huipils for as long as she has lived in San Miguel, which is decades. I first encountered this American artist through an exhibition of her work at the Bellas Artes—over-sized huipils made from cornstalks, film negatives, rose petals, CDs, book pages, clothing labels, tea bags, Zapatista bandanas, used paper coffee filters. The work was beautiful, political, feminist. Not long after, Lena was pointed out to me in a restaurant, unforgettable with her shock of pink hair, long gauzy skirt, and bright embroidered huipil. When we passed each other on the street, we'd smile, my halo of curly white hair nodding to her shock of pink. By the time I found her gallery, La Huipilista Artspace, dedicated to art made by women's hands on the theme of women's clothing, we felt we'd known each other forever.

Lena has told me that Indigenous women, when they were forbidden to speak their native languages by the colonizing Spaniards, invented ways of communicating with each other. They wove stories into the designs embroidered on their huipils, transforming their blouses into clandestine codices, fabric archives of religious beliefs, agricultural secrets, and community traditions. "No two huipils are exactly alike," she writes in *Whispers in the Thread*. "They served as markers for individual and for collective identity. They covered the body, simultaneously revealing and concealing cultural knowledge."

Secrets in plain view, masquerading as women's clothing.

Beth's huipil is more subtle than any I've seen. A pattern is woven into the cloth by varying the weave, fine to coarse to fine. Barely discernible symbols are embroidered in white on the finely woven panels. White-on-white flowers, perhaps. Or maybe faces. The front, shoulders, and hemline of the huipil seem embossed rather than embroidered, an effect closer to brocade.

I scour the internet for images of other white-on-white huipils. I find thousands intricately embroidered in bright colours, but none that are uniformly creamy, like this gift from Beth.

I try to be content with the mystery, with never knowing which village or which culture or which woman this pale brocade belonged to; with never deciphering the white symbol that appears to me now as neither a flower nor a face but a circle with eight radiating points, like a noonday sun.

Slender Threads

I HAVE BEEN TOSSING PHOTOGRAPHS. I DOUBT I WOULD HAVE had the courage to open my sixty years of albums if a catastrophic flood hadn't washed through our condo, forcing my hand.

Most pictures are easy to throw out: endless shots of birthday parties and weddings, school friends I haven't seen in half a century and wasn't close to at the time. Yet I keep a photo of the roses I wore in my hair for my first wedding; of Perdita, the tiny cat that adopted me in second-year university and lay on my tummy as it grew large and round with my first child. None of that is in the photograph, only the animal's sweet face, which recalls a whole world for me.

When Wayne's mother was dying—the swift, two-month downward spiral of stomach cancer—I pulled plastic grocery bags out from under her couch and used up a week of precious afternoons insisting she identify all the people in the pictures. I thought they would mean something to her sons and her grandchildren, but they don't. Photographs, I've come to believe, are only of interest to the person who was there for the taking: Proustian madeleines for our memories.

I pile up the salvaged photos with the intention of making one album of my life, the *Reader's Digest* version, but I cannot shake the notion that my children may want a visual record of where they came from, who they used to be. So I assemble an album for each of them, guessing at which images will hold meaning for them.

I have already given three of the children their albums, on their birthdays in January, March, and May. This morning I am setting aside photos for the last album, the one for my oldest son. He has the most pictures, being the first child, so the decisions are harder. Such dilemmas won't present themselves to our children. Their thousands of digital photos won't need a flood to be obliterated, just the tap of a finger.

I have a digital cache too: more than 26,000 images stored in the Cloud. I made a pact with myself to spend a few minutes every day among those too, deleting the non-essential. This week I culled 1,300, which leaves tens of thousands still to sort through.

I know what I am gaining by this exercise: storage space, both physical and virtual. My computer's memory can't take much more, and neither can our crawl-space shelves. But what am I losing? What future worlds of memory are dropping away every time I press Delete? Without these visual prompts, what stories will be forgotten forever?

Then again, what does it matter? When I'm gone, the stories will be gone too.

I email Beth and ask her to tell me the story of the white huipil. There is no reply, so I ask again. She responds to the second email, but not to the question. I imagine the stories she isn't telling me: She bought the huipil on a clandestine trip to Mexico, or she's never been to Mexico—the huipil was a gift from a travelling friend.

None of my imaginings are true, of course. She has been spending days poring through her lifetime of little leather appointment books, trying to pinpoint the year and the date on which she bought the hand-loomed blouse. And at last she does: January 4, 1978. Then she hauled out her atlas to find the places she visited on that trip. "I can pronounce the names," she writes to me, "but I am unable to spell them in a way that the atlas recognizes."

When I arrive at Beth's the following week, she has arranged two lawn chairs on the cement walk that leads from the driveway to her front steps. A construction project has rerouted traffic past her house: buses, transport trucks, every spewing vehicle imaginable. We wear our masks, and what with the mask-muffling, Beth's quiet voice, and all that engine noise, I worry we won't hear each other at all.

But the day is balmy and so we settle into our chairs, prepared to make the best of it. On the folding table between us is the atlas, as big as the table itself. Under the atlas, a photograph album, and on top, a small square of white paper with three names: Tijuana, Cancún, Chichén Itzá. In the atlas, Beth has not been able to find any of the places she visited with Jack, and no wonder. Cancún didn't exist when the atlas was published, although I find it on my iPhone, near the tip of the Yucatán Peninsula. Beth and Jack's winter vacation was in 1978, only four years after the tourist city was built, the beaches fringed almost overnight with high-rise hotels. At the time, the place still held vestiges of the fishermen's island it once was, surrounded by virgin forest. While they were there, Beth and Jack made a side trip to Chichén Itzá, a three-hour drive west on the Mérida highway.

"I wanted to see the Toltec sculptures," says Beth. "They were so like the sculptures of Henry Moore."

We thumb through her photograph album—thick, sticky pages that hold the photographs in place, protected by a glassine flap, exactly like the albums I've been culling except that Beth's album is intact. There she is in front of a Mayan pyramid, a bit fuller in the face but completely recognizable, her eyes refusing the camera, an unwelcome interruption to whatever thoughts she is entertaining.

In 2006, after an eighty-year-old American woman fell to her death while climbing up the Temple of Kukulkán, the ruins at Chichén Itzá were closed to the public. Now they can be seen only from a distance. Tourists can look but not touch.

How lucky Beth and Jack were, almost alone on the site. Beth hiked to the top of every temple. In 1989, when I visited Palenque, another ancient Mayan city in the Yucatán, visitors could still roam free. As my son and I laboriously climbed up the Temple of the Inscriptions, a Mayan man with flowing black hair ran barefoot past us down the steep, narrow steps, an unforgettable tranquility on his beautiful face. This was not exercise and definitely not a tourist entertainment. I had the impression that for this Mayan, the visit to the temple was a pilgrimage.

Beth bought the white huipil in one of the thatched-roof booths on the fringes of Chichén Itzá. At least, that is her best guess. She remembers a weaver with a backstrap loom, but the specifics of this particular purchase elude her.

At home, I look up Mayan huipils again, and this time stumble on the significance of their colours. The Mayan palette of four dyes represents the four types of corn, and by extension the four elements of the body: red for blood, black for eyes and hair, yellow for muscle, and white for bones. The colours also represent the four directions of the winds: red for east, black for west, white for north, and yellow for south. So the creamy cloth of my huipil speaks of the south, of sun and corn. The white embroidery is the north; it is hope and promise and spirituality—all that is untouchable.

I search the symbols too, but find nothing that fits precisely with the embroidered images on my huipil. Circular embroidered patterns reflect the timeless round of planting, flowering, fruiting, and collecting seed to start the growing cycle all over again. Perhaps the embossed circles on my huipil are not suns but flowers after all, offerings to the gods and goddesses in hopes of ensuring a good harvest.

I am aware that I am not seeing what is there so much as choosing what I want to see.

Finally I find a short, obscure reference to the huipils of Cobán, a city in the coffee-growing hills at the centre of Guatemala. The huipils from that region are typically made of undyed cloth, embroidered in white.

Cobán is a long way from Chichén Itzá—a fifteen-hour drive at least, and much longer in 1978, when all the roads were rough. Perhaps a Guatemalan daughter married a Mexican and took her mother's backstrap loom north with her. Perhaps a salesman bought up huipils as he travelled through the mountains of Central America, then displayed them at his stall on the fringes of Chichén Itzá.

Or perhaps this huipil came from the loom of a restless Mayan woman who decided one day to break with tradition, toss aside her coloured threads, and emboss the creamy woven fabric with hopeful white.

This is how we fashion stories: weaving together the slender threads of what is known with what we imagine, what we hope.

The Pleasure of Being Necessary

IN AN ESSAY PUBLISHED IN 2017 IN *THE NEW YORKER*, TONI Morrison wrote about working as a cleaner when she was a child. She was thrilled to have her own money to spend on ice cream, movies, and jacks, but she always gave half her earnings to her mother, her contribution to daily expenses, which brought young Toni a different kind of thrill.

"The pleasure of being necessary to my parents was profound," she wrote. "I was not like the children in folktales: burdensome mouths to feed, nuisances to be corrected, problems so severe that they were abandoned to the forest. I had a status that routine chores did not provide in my house—and it earned me a slow smile, an approving nod from an adult. Confirmation that I was adultlike, not childlike."

My own parents were not poor. My father moved us to Brazil, where we lived in relative privilege while he set up a factory and trained its workers. Still, at the age of ten, I hired myself out as an interpreter, accompanying expat women to the markets to shop. At our little English-language school, I set up a concession stand where students could buy snacks at recess; I donated the profits to the library to buy books. Later, back in our village in Canada, my sisters and I made the rounds of our great-aunts and -uncles and their elderly friends every Saturday to clean their houses.

From a very young age, I knew the feeling of being essential, if only in small ways. But at the other end of life—over the hill, as they say—it is easy to feel unnecessary. I can dole out money, but how often am I called upon to perform a service that someone else can't be paid to do?

My mother's sister lived to a few months shy of her one hundredth birthday. She passed the last fifteen years of her life in a retirement facility, and for at least ten of those she'd say to me every time I visited, "Why am I still alive? No one needs me. I have nothing to do, no reason to live."

"I'm glad you're still alive," I'd say lamely, clearly not the reassurance she was looking for.

Beth grew up at a time when children were essential—to look after siblings (there was no such thing as daycare), to hoe the garden (it took all hands to grow enough food for a large family), to run errands for a mother strained by the demands of that same large family, with no vacuum or dishwasher or washer/dryer or microwave to help.

Yet when I ask if she felt necessary as a child, she pauses for a very long time, as if trying to figure out what on earth I might mean. "It never occurred to me," she says finally. "From a very young age, at least by five, we had helpers and maids in the house because my father hoped that would free my mother to enter the activities of an editor's social life, which was very lively."

Is this finding of pleasure in being necessary an innate quality? Clearly not, since Beth grew up to be a tireless volunteer with the deaf, in the arts, with veterans. Her contributions were so notable she was awarded both the Queen Elizabeth II Diamond Jubilee Medal and the Sovereign's Medal for Volunteers.

My mother never won any medals. She was not a particularly social person, but even so, she was always giving, unconsciously making herself necessary to the people around her. Towards the end of her life she received a letter from a woman who had grown up in our village. As a child, she used to visit my mother, who made clothes for her dolls and cut up sandwiches into tiny squares for doll picnics. Listening, when the moment called for that. The woman wrote that, through those years, she was being abused, and my mother's kitchen was a safe place for her.

Sometimes we are necessary without knowing it.

In Mexico, where I live half the year, I feel needed in a way I don't in Canada. There are endless ways to contribute, both within the expat community and among Mexicans. The migrants who ride La Bestia to the American border—the long train whistle pierces my sleep every night—need money, clothes, shampoo and soap, backpacks. Audubon de México needs help clearing the invasive water hyacinths that are smothering the reservoir and destroying the local fishery; they need angels to pry away the parasitic plants that are strangling the mesquite and huizache trees. And my friends in Mexico need me. There aren't a lot of us, which intensifies our connection. I need their love and support, and they need mine.

There is a stillness to Beth, a forever-ness that feels essential to me. It's the same feeling I had around my mother, who tried her best to calm me, to rein in my enthusiasms, my habit of wearing every thought and feeling on my sleeve—taming, just a little, that rambunctious, rippling rapid of a girl. I'm still a bit like that, quick to enthusiasms that can suck the oxygen from a room. Perhaps that's why I'm drawn to Beth's unruffled depths, the all but imperceptible flow of her emotions, occasionally glimpsed in the flutter of a hand or a momentary cloud across the eyes.

Beth's stillness is not the stillness at the eye of a storm. More like the apparent stillness of a bee in a flower that you only notice when you stop your frantic weeding and get down on your hands and knees to peer deep into the folds of the petals, where the bee is quietly tumbling, humming softly as it goes about its singular, essential work.

Grow Here

ON THE MORNING OF OUR LAST VISIT IN MAY, I AM UP WITH the sun and outside in the garden. I write "garden," but it hardly deserves the name. I used to work a garden that stretched across two acres. Now I have a miniature facsimile along one side of our condo terrace: two Swiss chard plants instead of two ten-foot rows; a single hosta, one astilbe, a lone coral bell where once great swaths flowed down from the woods to our stone house in the country.

Still, the pleasure I feel with my hands in the earth is undiminished. To say that the act grounds me is inadequate. There is something timeless about digging a hollow in soil, spreading the roots of a seedling, settling it in place, wishing it well. In an early photo of me, I am standing in my grandmother's garden hefting a watering can. Another watering can of the same design but newer vintage stands outside our door now. It barely comes up to my knees, but every time I water the daffodils, the pansies, the geraniums, the fall asters, I am that little girl, my own grandmother, my granddaughter too, who called me yesterday to ask how to plant her first garden. I am that first woman who plucked a seed from a withering plant, kept it dry and clean until the soil warmed and moistened again, then pushed it in, saying, "Please. Grow here." I am the child of my children's children's children, who will do the same, I hope.

Many older women have found solace and inspiration in their

gardens. I think of Gertrude Jekyll, the British artist who, when her eyes grew too dim for her to continue painting, planted a living palette of colour. I used to see the cycle of seed to plant to fruit to seed as especially suited to the latter stage of life, an affirmation of the inevitability of decline and the comforting continuity of a seed.

I think differently now. Gardens need their gardeners. When a person has left the working world and all its must-dos, when we drift to the margins of society, the garden plot is still there, calling, *Come weed! Please water! Look at me now, while I'm at my best.*

At the back of her historic row house in Portsmouth Village, now part of Kingston, Beth created a serene Japanese garden, all white stone and perfectly placed, gracefully leaning plants in particular shades of green.

The front yard of the split-level bungalow where she lives now has those two glorious maple trees and a foundation bed of perennials. Except in the dead of winter, she always has potted flowers on her little front stoop and by the garage, and another on her back deck. Even so, grass predominates. "This place doesn't inspire my creative soul," she admits without resentment.

So I'm surprised when Beth greets me at the door one June afternoon with the exclamation "I'm giving myself a garden!"

She takes me by the hand and leads me past the garage and through the gate into the backyard, to her little tool shed that looks like a cottage. There the grass has been peeled away, the soil worked up, and a few plants bedded in. Hostas. Ferns. Kitchen herbs.

I am astonished by the little garden, but more than that, by how well Beth knows herself and the effort she has made to fulfill her own needs.

"If people would just listen to their soul," she says with a smile, "they will find the solution to anything."

Up and Over, Up and Over

BETH MIMES A STITCHING MOTION, THEN SAYS ABRUPTLY, "Wait here!" and sprints out of the room.

"I'm calling it 'Sahara,'" she says, holding out a thin white cardboard rectangle the size of a large postcard. The bottom half is covered with fine chain stitch in shades of beige, pink, and tan; the top half is bare except for a starter blue thread of sky.

"Morocco. From one of Gillian's photographs."

I'm gobsmacked. What other secret passions have I yet to discover in this friend of mine? Beth doesn't use a pattern or sketch the piece first with coloured pencil. She doesn't even follow the photograph very closely. She points to a stitched shadow in the sand dune that angles off in an odd direction. "I need to tear this out. It isn't right."

I think of the women in the Greek village of Rhodini, where my first husband, our toddler son, and I lived for a month in our VW van, parked on the beach. Every evening, women young and old gathered on the stone stoops of their houses, built around the village well, each with a cloth in one hand, a needle with bright thread in the other. They laughed and talked as their needles flew—or, more correctly, they embroidered as they chatted, hardly glancing at the cloth, the cadence from their lips caught in the rhythm of their fingers.

The Mexican women in the town where we pass our winters sit in doorways too, embroidering through the day, tortilla cloths and table runners, napkins. Señora Juana, who lived at the end of our street when we first arrived in San Miguel, would pull aside her kitchen curtain now and then to sell handmade tortillas; one day she laid embroidered cloths on the bench in front of her house. The tortillas and the embroidery, both handwork to fill every spare moment.

I no longer embroider, but when we moved to Brazil and our Christmas decorations went missing, my mother came home one day with needles, embroidery thread, and a roll of red felt that she cut into Christmas stockings. She laid squares of green, white, blue, and black felt on the table, too, encouraging the four of us girls to cut out Christmas trees, tiny felt gifts, icicles to dribble from the top of the stocking, gingerbread houses, stars, Santa sleighs, whatever we could imagine. The felt icons were glued to the stocking, then held in place with cross-stitch, chain stitch, stem stitch, satin stitch, French knots. I remember my mother's young hands, not the rope-veined, arthritic hands they became, guiding my small fingers up and over, teaching me the chain stitch that spells my name on the stocking that I still hang up at Christmas.

"Here!" Beth thrusts a roll of black cloth at me. I've never seen her so impish. "Open this!"

I untie the cord of purplish pink wool and unroll the black cloth at my feet. Embroidery thread: dozens upon dozens of packets arranged in a rainbow from purple, blue, green through yellow, orange, red.

She tells me about her grandmother Harriett, who always had tatting bobbins or knitting needles or a crochet hook in hand, shaping coloured threads into some useful object for the home, as women have done for centuries.

"All women needed to protect their quiet, respite moments from the ongoing demands of a multitude of tasks, and the ever-present needs of their children," Beth writes in *My Journey to One Hundred*, the book she is working on now. "How clever was this needle moat! How legitimate those quiet corners!"

Beth is rubbing her right hand, as if it aches with the bone-memory of all those generations of women's work. With hardly a break in the conversation, she slips an elastic support over her fingers and tightens the Velcro strap. She stares at her fingers. "They have a mind of their own now," she says, smiling. She pulls the contraption off and lays her hand on her knee, fingers flat. Within seconds, they curl into a cup.

She slips the support back on and I think she's going to pick up her needle and thread, that the two of us will become *pláticas* like those Mexican women, hands and tongues weaving a fabric of shared lives. But no. She lifts up another small piece of white cardboard, this one called "Juno Beach." Drifts of chain-stitch sand give way to green, blue, grey waves that stretch to the borders of the cardboard. In the bottom left, a small figure with thin black legs stands in a fluffy white coat and black hat.

Beth.

Not a Birthday Gift

BETH TURNS A HUNDRED AND ONE TODAY. SHE DECIDED LAST year that one hundred would be her turning point. She would begin to count backwards from there.

"Happy ninety-ninth!" I say when I call her in the early afternoon.

"No gifts!" she told me last week. "If you bring a gift, I won't let you in the house!"

Because her birthday falls on a Wednesday, our usual day, we agree to skip this week. I do, in fact, have a gift for her, but if I bring it next week, it will be just one of the many gifts we give each other whenever we feel like it, not a birthday gift at all.

I love giving gifts. For the days, sometimes months, that I am searching for the perfect gift, the person on the receiving end lives large in my heart and mind. Normally I cruise shops and event listings; in this lockdown year, I visit the cornucopia of the internet. Will it fit? Is it the right colour? Is this something she'd like? Will it bring a smile to her face?

So when a close friend had a birthday a few weeks ago and declared, "No birthday lunch, no gifts, nada," her words were a cleaver to my heart. She said, *No gifts*, but what I heard was, *Don't think of me. Don't hold me close, even for a day*. I asked if we could have dinner—a games night with our partners. Sure, she said, so long as no one says, "Happy birthday." My granddaughter, who also has a birthday this month, does want gifts, bless her heart, but what she wants most of all is money. I know the childhood joy of coming upon a folded twenty-dollar bill inside a card, but what is that compared with the deep delight of feeling truly known, of lifting a book twenty years from now and recalling the hands that touched hers in the giving? My son on his birthday this year sent around an email to family and friends: No visits. No party. No gifts. Instead, he was donating his birthday-party fund to a local food bank and hoped others would do the same.

I'm in favour of donating to food banks; I used to grow extra vegetables in my summer garden to give to the hungry. And I'm no fan of lavish parties of the kind that Toller Cranston, the figure skater, used to throw in San Miguel, rooms thick with perfumed, buzzing bodies, tables groaning with cakes leaking chocolate, ice cream cones stuck into the top, Smarties thick as gravel on the tablecloth, a Hansel and Gretel fantasy. But I do love to celebrate. I love the music, the flower-garden dresses and crisp shirts, the dancing, the laughter, all the people you love and who love you in the same room or park or restaurant patio, like a posse of good fairies bestowing their best wishes.

I was looking for a birthday gift for Wayne—thank goodness he allows me to carry him large in my heart—when I found the perfect gift for Beth: a silver case, smaller than a business card holder, bigger than a locket, although it opens like one and invites a secret cache. The front swirls with delicate Art Nouveau etching, perfect for a woman born in 1920. Best of all, the initial in the centre is either a *B* or an *R*—there is so much filigree I can't tell which, but no matter, both are appropriate.

Inside the case, I place a row of strike-anywhere matches and, tucked into the other side, a small piece of sandpaper for striking. I imagine Beth carrying this gift to the lantern that hangs from her back deck, imagine her opening the case, lifting out a match tipped in red (her favourite colour), and drawing it swiftly over the coarse, pebbly sandpaper, lifting the flame to the wick of the blue-green candle. It doesn't matter how she actually uses it, if she uses it at all, or if it lies in a drawer for the rest of her life—the thought of this case in her hand brings me joy.

On the day I bring Beth her gift, a hand-painted Mexican plate is waiting on the hall bench. "I am laying things out, and whoever happens by, if they love it, it is theirs."

This makes me think of the day after the funeral of Wayne's mother, when all her jewellery was laid on top of her dresser, awaiting her grandchildren. And the day after my father's death, when we four daughters took small round stickers, a different colour for each of us, and wandered around the house fixing a red, yellow, green, or blue circle on the things we loved. We figured that if, at the end of the day, a vase or a chair or a mirror had more than one coloured dot, the horse-trading could begin. But there was very little of that; we each loved different things.

I have wrapped Beth's not-a-birthday gift in paper that looks as though it could be on her wall, a swirl of cream and endless blues with flashes of gold. Beth takes the parcel from me and leads the way into the living room. I note again the attention she pays to dressing—today, slim black slacks and a fine-knit white top, red shoes. She has told me how, each morning, she takes the temperature of the day and her mood, carefully selecting each piece of clothing from her closet and laying it on the bed, considering how the colours, patterns, and shapes interact. Accessories are chosen to match or contrast. Today, a bright shawl and a black stone necklace, both from Morocco. Long-ago gifts from Gillian.

"I will use this," Beth says, clicking open the silver case, running her fingers over the red match heads. "Any ritual you perform builds trust in a belief, and it's been hard for me to believe Gillian is still around." When she looks up at me, I see tears in her eyes.

A Numbers Game

"WHAT AGE ARE YOU?" I ASK BETH AFTER SHE HAS POURED THE fennel tea and passed the grapes and gingersnaps.

She looks at me as if I've lost my mind. I know she's a hundred and one. Then it dawns on her what I mean.

"I had a hard time accepting that I was a hundred," she says finally. "It's such a huge number! I wanted to stay ninety-nine."

To Beth I admit my own peculiar relationship with the number of years I've been on this planet. I love prime numbers, so at some point in my thirties I decided to stick with them. I was 37 for a few years, then 41, 43, 47, 53. Somewhere around the halfway point between two prime numbers I'd shift to the next, so I was 47 for three years, then suddenly 53 for another three. Only one person noticed, a journalist who interviewed me around the release of a new book. "I need to check your age," he said when he called later to verify some facts. "You told me you were fifty-three, but you can't be if you were born in 1949. Why did you say you're older than you are?"

"Age is just a number," I say to Beth, who I know will understand. "For a long time, people never really knew the year they were born or their age. In some parts of the world, they still don't. You are an infant, a child, an adult, an old person."

Beth laughs, then leans close as if what she is about to tell me is a really big secret. "When my children were young, I was allowed to be thirty-nine as long as I was able to swim from the cottage to an island in the lake and back."

"How old do you feel now?"

My mother, right to the end, said she felt eighteen; it was a surprise every time she looked in the mirror. "Who is that old lady?" she'd say.

"Most days I feel seventy-four," Beth says. "That's how old I was when my husband died. That's when I entered this new stage, where I still am now."

Ikigai

BETH AND I ARE DRINKING TEA FROM JAPANESE CUPS, DELICATE bowls that she brings into the living room on a small round rattan tray, ducking under a short curtain tacked across the doorway from the kitchen. The curtain, she explains, is a *noren*, a staple in the decor of Japanese homes and businesses. These fabric dividers have hung over entrances in Japan since the eighth century, helping to keep houses cool in summer and holding in the heat in winter. Unlike the curtains in Canadian houses, which can be drawn and pulled back along rods, the *noren* is a permanent separator of spaces. And in Beth's case, a constant reminder of all that she loves about Japan and the Japanese: the delicacy, the tradition, the care. *Noren* are traditionally handwoven from cotton or linen and coloured with natural dyes. Beth's is a beautiful handmade collage of fabric, five squares of red-and-gold floral designs alternating with black squares, the whole thing framed in black, the fabric light enough to waft in the breeze of her passing. When I enter Beth's house, the *noren* is the first thing I see, a signal that this is no ordinary place.

"I really thought I should have been born in Japan," she says. "If it weren't for the First World War, my father would have been teaching there."

The idea of Japan planted itself early in Beth's imagination, but it wasn't until she took a course in Chinese and Japanese art at the

Ontario College of Art that she became entranced. She felt an urge to learn the Japanese tea ceremony, and in Toronto she found a Japanese tea master to induct her into its rituals.

"You come to it as an aesthetic experience. You wear your kimono. You sit on a special wooden bench until you are invited in. Once the invitation is offered, you stop at a hollowed stone filled with fresh, clear water, and with the bamboo ladle, you wash your hands; with your fingers, you lift water to cleanse your lips. Only then are you prepared for the ceremony. You climb through a very small door. This automatically requires a gesture of bowing, of humility. I wasn't able to sit exactly the way the Japanese sit, so they gave me a small block, about three inches high, to help me."

The Japanese tea ceremony is a manifestation of aesthetic appreciation. She describes how the host presents the tea bowl to each guest in turn. The front of the bowl always faces the guest, who picks up the bowl with the right hand and places it in the left palm, then bows once and raises the tea bowl to the host, making sure the front of the bowl is now facing the host. Finally, the guest bows to express gratitude and respect for the four ideals of tea: harmony, respect, purity, and tranquility.

She pauses.

"The tea ceremony has lingered with me. It was an indelibly moving experience. At about that time, my youngest son, Bruce, died of cancer. The group of women I was learning with responded by having a special tea ceremony, with special writing on the wall, a vase of special flowers gathered while the dew was still on the petals . . ."

A year later, Beth finally visited Japan. She was eighty-six. She studied for the trip as for an exam, reading and talking with friends who had been there. But nothing, she says in a hushed tone, prepared her for the impact of Kyoto.

"It was like going through a huge portal. I was home."

Each day for fourteen days, she visited a different temple. "Gradually one Buddha is becoming important to me," she wrote about the trip. "Yakushi Nyorai, the healing Buddha. His right hand is raised, palm facing forward, as if silently saying, 'Fear not.' In his left hand, he holds a small amphora containing healing spirits."

Between temples, she lingered in gardens that were the epitome of silence and beauty.

> There is a garden with a pond, moss, shaped trees and bushes. Then there are large spaces of raked, patterned sand and, always a miracle, a well-placed stone. I sat and watched a man wrapping a stone with black cord. He wrapped slowly and carefully, as if it were a meditation. When he was finished, I asked him where he was going to place it, and he said, "In a pathway, so people will know they can go no further." Imagine—not a sign. A carefully wrapped stone.

I take a deep breath. I would put up a sign. Gently worded, I hope, but still a sign. I think of the woman who every few days appears at my gate in Mexico. She slides one hand between the iron uprights, offering a neat green packet of lemongrass, the thin leaves folded into themselves, one leaf wrapped around the packet to hold it tight. To make my tea, I unwrap one leaf a time, fold it neatly in the bottom of the cup, and pour in the boiling water.

I've had so many teachers, yet I still have so much to learn.

"The Japanese are given to moving gently and quietly," Beth says. "No matter what they are doing, even picking tiny green sprouts from the raked sand where they're not supposed to grow, always honouring the earth, the air, the pathways. There is much in me that needs that gentle way."

Beth had begun her professional life as an occupational therapist in a Quebec military hospital. It was later, working with long-term patients in Toronto, that she began to play records, read stories, and bring art materials into the ward. The patients' response to the paints, pencils, and clay led her to train as an art therapist. For many years she had a private practice in Toronto, with periodic teaching stints at the Ontario College of Art and Design and Concordia University in Montreal. She officially retired from Concordia at the age of sixty-eight. "I spent all my first pension cheque taking people out for lunch!"

That year, she and Jack moved to Delta, Ontario, where they built a house on a twenty-acre parcel of trees and Lower Beverley Lake shoreline that met "fingertip to fingertip" with her family's cottage property. She and Jack sat on lawn chairs placed in imaginary rooms mapped out with string in an open field. "We moved a ladder to different positions to locate our potential view. We kept shifting the string of our outside walls to coax sunshine through our imagined windows. Then we drove in the stakes and invited the neighbours for a housewarming inside the string rooms. A happy, crazy beginning!"

When the house was built, sun did indeed pour through the windows, the garage held the cars, the antique boats, and Jack's workshop, and Beth had a room of her own with tall bookshelves and French doors that opened to the lake. They mowed a labyrinth in the field, wildflowers edging the path where they would walk in the evenings.

They spent only four years together in that house. After Jack died, Beth sold the lakeside property and moved into Kingston, where she took up other passions—poetry, dance, writing, art. A local psychiatrist, working with a surge of servicemen suffering from PTSD, invited Beth to join her as an art therapist. A film was made; they organized exhibitions of the veterans' artwork and brought in speakers to raise public awareness of PTSD.

When Beth was ninety-seven, she was part of an experimental art therapy treatment program for soldiers at Kingston's military base.

"We had a room at the back of the Anglican church, with a beautiful long table set with art supplies. I'd ask everyone to stand and look at the colours in their pastel box, pick out one that spoke to them, then take that one colour and make a line that felt right. 'Now you have one colour and one line,' I'd say. 'Are you happy to leave the line as it is, or are there other colours you might like to add to it? Take your colours and play until you feel you've said what you want to say.' They would just dive right in. Some of the telltale aspects of their anxiety or fatigue began to be visible. When everyone stopped, we put the drawings up on a board. Through the afternoon, each of them would have the opportunity for a one-on-one talk with me about the image they'd made."

Later that spring, a case of shingles put Beth's working life on pause. The next year, her daughter died and Covid hit, and art became her own lifeline.

"My itches are sizable," Beth says out of the blue. At first I think she's about to tell me of some awful ongoing malady, but no, she means her passions, all the interests that obsess her. "I have deep wells of passion. They are the motivating force of my life."

She falls silent for a moment, then says, "Do you know that in Japan they don't have a word for 'retire,' even though most people leave their official work around the age of sixty?"

"And in North America," I counter, "we don't have a word for *ikigai*."

"What's that?"

"*Ee-kee-guy*. It's like an all-encompassing concept of work—what you are good at and what supports you financially, but also what you love to do and what is good for the world."

Beth looks thoughtful. Our first conversations in this year of walking and talking were about retirement, how it can feel like a dead end instead of an opening door.

"Many people reach retirement never having thought about what has given them pleasure or satisfaction in their life," Beth says. "What can take them into the next stage. They don't realize they have no need of a boss or a job description. Any number of activities are self-initiated. I can't believe how much has happened between 1988, when I officially retired from teaching art therapy at Concordia, and now—dance, embroidery, my collages—clusters of activity, each one different, yet in a way they are part of one long, continuous journey. Every day, at every age, you wake up, your eyes open, your whole being opens, and off you go!"

I grin. "That's *ikigai*!"

Ebb Tide

FOR TWO MONTHS OF THE YEAR—FROM JULY 22 UNTIL SEPTEMBER 25—Beth and I are exactly thirty years apart. This year, she is a hundred and one and I am seventy-one, both prime numbers.

I have looked forward to this liminal time of mathematical symmetry. I imagined seeing Beth more often, our conversations deepening. Instead, we hardly see each other at all. As Covid cases take a summer holiday, visitors flock to Beth's door. And I can't join the roster even if there is room.

I have a spear in my skull, or at least that's what it feels like. For weeks I've had an intensifying, unremitting headache that has erased all thought from my brain, all will from my body. Two weeks after Beth's birthday, I finally get the diagnosis: giant cell arteritis (GCA). The cells in the walls of the temporal artery that feeds my eye and my brain have grown to many times their normal size. My right temple is so swollen the specialist can't find a pulse.

"This is not a diagnosis I want to make," the doctor says to me before he performs the ultrasound that is the defining test for this mysterious vascular disease that as yet has no known cause.

I am lying flat on the examining table. I push down the pain and respond brightly, "Well, it is what it is!"

"This is *not* a diagnosis anyone wants," he repeats, his voice even.

I am beginning to understand. GCA has changed everything: what I eat, how I spend my day—mostly managing pills and trying to exercise—but especially my sense of the future. I had always assumed I would carry on at least as long as the grandmother I most resemble, who lived well into her nineties. Now I'm not so sure. I read everything I can find about this strange, rare form of vasculitis, especially its impact on the life expectancy of its victims. Most studies estimate eight years. One says, on average, three.

Damon Galgut, in his novel *A Strange Room*, describes a journey as "a gesture inscribed in space, it vanishes even as it's made." The same can be said of a life, I think, my confidence in longevity evaporating. I am a wavelet making for shore, the waters closing behind me as if I'd never been, nothing but a thin thread of foam left on the water, to be disturbed by another's passing.

I find this new thought oddly comforting. My presence in the world, which has often felt heavy with intent, with need and desire, does not have to be such a burden after all.

I am. I was. A simple shift in tense.

Repose

I SPEND MY DAYS NOW IN REPOSE, LYING ON THE COUCH, napping on the bed. "Repose" also means death—a body laid out in repose—but I avoid that definition. Beth uses the word in its oldest sense: to be calm, quiet, at peace. During the few times through the late summer that we manage to get together, she urges me to strive for mental rest, a liberation from stress, anxiety, turbulent emotion. A respite. A steadiness of heart that is immune to what is going on around it. Tranquility. Serenity. Repose.

When anti-inflammatories and painkillers finally make it possible for me to invite Beth to visit, she reads me a passage from May Sarton that she has copied into her notebook. Until I fell ill, we were reading other writers too, but we always came back to this poet who so eloquently explored love, creativity, and the conflict of mind and body in her poems, yet in her memoirs on aging and illness became curmudgeonly in her complaints.

"She had a deep need for solitude and quiet," Beth says. "But I find no sense of repose in what she wrote."

I pass the time searching the internet for repose paintings. I recognize a painting of a young woman reclining on a plush couch, by Édouard Manet. I marvel at how the artist has captured the complete relaxation of her body, her arms languorous, fingers splayed limply on the fabric of the settee, legs outstretched, her whole body slouched, even her dress hanging loose. Berthe Morisot, Manet's sister-in-law, was often his model, but the painting isn't a portrait of Berthe so much as of a state of being. In contrast, the painting that hangs on the wall behind the woman's head is a frenetic swirl of colour, dark, thundering waves breaking against a murky horizon. This comes closer to what it feels like to be me.

In between naps and medical appointments, I search lazily for other meanings of "repose," and happen upon its meaning in geology: the period between eruptions of a volcano.

I sometimes feel that my life moves from eruption to eruption, scarcely any repose in between. Beth, on the other hand, seems always in repose—calm, composed, fully herself. I close my computer and stretch out on the couch, working to relax one body part after the other, from the tips of my toes to the place where the spear splits my skull.

Periodically when I was an adolescent, I'd run a fever for no apparent reason and be felled by a peculiar fatigue that would send me to my bed for the better part of a week. "Rest," my mother would say, stroking my forehead. My mother was a nurse. When I'd object that I couldn't rest, I had too much to do, she'd gently press me back against the sheets, saying, "Rest is an activity too."

Certainties

CERTAINTY IS WHAT BETH BUILDS HER LIFE AROUND. THOSE things she can't change. The way the knuckles of her right hand dislocate so that every so often she has to tap that hand against her thigh to realign the bones. The shingles that set the left side of her torso on fire almost four years ago and still make her say by suppertime, *Okay, that's it for today*.

These certainties may require something of her now and then, but they exercise no power over her. They aren't disabilities or complaints; they are fixities. Truths around which she freely moves.

I strive now to do the same.

Rearranging the Crystals

BETH HAS VERTIGO.

"I can't look up," she says. "The doctor said to keep my face either directly ahead or down." So instead of looking up at her rack of clothing to choose today's outfit—black capris, red shoes, and a long, silky blouse that Mondrian would envy—she felt the hems at eye level and let her fingers travel up to the hanger, her gaze safely fixed straight ahead.

She follows her doctor's advice to the last detail, but she also believes in physiotherapy, so I'm not surprised when she tells me she's been having physio to rearrange the crystals in her ears. The most common type of vertigo occurs when small crystals of calcium come loose in the inner ear. The therapist has Beth lie flat on her back with her head lower than her body and tells her to follow his finger with her eyes, a subtle way of manipulating her head to encourage the crystals to move within the ear canal.

"It's not so bad," Beth says, brushing the topic aside, although she suffers from the treatments and is often so nauseated afterwards that she has to cancel our visit.

Beth and I do not indulge in what my husband calls organ recitals: mournful tales of all that hurts and why. We both have less than robust bodies and we resent the time we spend managing them. Last week her eyes were swollen almost closed.

"Allergies?" I asked.

"I don't have allergies," she said without energy, her voice raspier than usual.

New maladies come and go, but old injuries never seem to go away. My delicate spine, from falling backwards off the baseball bleachers. Beth's delicate back, from turning the mattress when her mother was dying of cancer, wrenching a muscle that still bothers her seventy years later.

Beth has thirty years on me, but already I can see that the body, like an old car, will need more and more maintenance to keep it on the road. Even at my age, the list of pings and knocks is long—longer than ever since GCA entered my life. We make a point of not allowing that doleful chorus into our brief time together. Instead, we laugh about our favourite ailments. I tell her about my "paradoxical vocal cords" and "redundant colon."

"Perfect for a writer!" she says with a chuckle.

By the time I get to my "exploding head syndrome," whereby I'm awakened in the night by sudden booming sounds, sometimes a shout or a cry or the sharp *ring-a-ding-ding* of a vintage telephone, all of it in my head, we are laughing so hard that tears are racing down our cheeks.

Beth looks steadfastly at my knees, still chuckling. "I don't mind keeping my head down for a while."

Cheek to Cheek

AT THE END OF EVERY VISIT, BETH AND I REACH OUR ARMS WIDE to each other in a Covid air hug. But I leave for Mexico tomorrow. This will be our last visit until spring, and so, without discussion, we move closer and wrap our arms tight around each other's bodies. We sense the length of those 180 days that we will be apart and press our bodies close.

Gently.

Beth is a delicate bird in my arms. She pads herself up nicely with flowing tops and down vests, but when we hug, my fingers fall into the curving hollows of her spine. It's all I can do not to register my alarm. Over the past few years, shingles and grief have stripped flesh from her bones.

My body is shape-shifting too. The corticosteroids enlisted to suppress the inflammation in my temporal artery have brought with them a nasty cohort of side effects. I rarely sleep more than a couple of hours. The capillaries under my skin burst at the slightest touch; my arms and legs are a map of bruises, islands intent on becoming dark continents. And yet the headache remains. I call her Hedda the Headache, my constant companion.

Already this supposed cure is carving away my thunder thighs and shrinking my lard-ass. The boys on the bus should see me now; they'd have to dredge their sludgy brains for some other nickname.

Moonface, perhaps, for as my bum-cheeks slim, my face balloons. I can feel my face-cheeks jiggle as I climb the stairs. A pad of soft jelly slathers my belly. Last week, a strange loose sac appeared under my chin. My dragonfly necklace, which usually drapes towards my cleavage, barely stretches around my neck. This morning I couldn't find my clavicles under a fresh flow of—what? Fluid? Fat?

Women's bodies are constantly changing. Breasts bud. Fill. Shrink. Sag. Bellies swell and flatten with the phases of the moon. Wombs ripen and drain. Tissues plump and desiccate. And not just women's bodies. Every living thing evolves through a cycle from the dawn of itself to its demise, physical structures changing minutely from day to day. No one is exempt. Fat accumulates as metabolism slows. Hair goes missing. Gums pull back from teeth. Skin loses elasticity. Tissues weaken. Muscles melt away. Even eyeballs sag.

I adapted as my cervix made its run for fresh air, as a loop of my small intestine buried itself in the femoral artery canal, as my bowels lost the will to move, as the delicate cauliflower alveoli of my lungs clogged with mucus florets. Through it all, I remained my familiar wide-hipped, wasp-waisted, square-jawed, widely smiling self.

But who is this thick-necked, apple-cheeked, bow-lipped woman in the mirror? My eyes—"your beautiful almond eyes," my grandmother used to say—have shrivelled to hazelnuts.

I am dismayed by this swift metamorphosis. *Don't be vain,* I hear my mother say. But it's not only that. I miss *me.* Will the woman I used to see in the mirror come back when all this is over? Will it ever be over? And what is happening, really? Am I taking on water like a sinking ship? Can fat actually migrate from bum to jowl?

Both, it turns out. Corticosteroids cause a body to hang on to fluid. They also trigger lipodystrophy—the accumulation of fat in unusual places. I reach around and palpate the top of my back. Buffalo hump! I adjust my calorie intake downwards and add upper back, neck, and chin exercises to my ever-lengthening daily regimen.

It is unwise to read too much, especially on the internet. The sites I visit promise that these side effects will reverse themselves when I stop the medication, but I haven't yet started the tortoise-slow weaning that my doctor says could last two years or more. I'll still have my moon face when I see Beth in the spring.

I lean away from her without leaving her arms. "Do you miss your former self?"

She shrugs. "I will miss *you*," she says, running her fingers down my fatty back. "I will miss our walks. Our conversations."

"We can't walk together, but we can talk," I say without conviction. "I can call you from Mexico. We'll send emails. Write letters. Zoom."

She gives me a long look. We both know it's not the same.

Nothing is ever the same.

One Hundred and Two

Seventy-Two

Please Write

OUR MONTHS AROUND THE TEAPOT ARE BEHIND US. IT IS WINTER; we must make do with weekly phone calls. In between, we write letters that masquerade as emails.

Beth has been sending letters across oceans and mountains most of her life. Her most significant correspondence was during the Second World War, when she met a young conscientious objector named Jim at a privately endowed psychiatric hospital in Baltimore, Maryland. He was waiting to be called up as a United States Army medic and she was fulfilling her first clinical placement in occupational therapy. It was the summer of 1942. Beth and Jim would often bump into each other on the paths between hospital buildings or in the cafeteria. Then the call-up came and suddenly the tall, dark, slender young man with the soft Tennessee accent was gone.

Beth returned to Toronto and took a job in a travel agency while she waited for a posting to the new Sainte-Anne-de-Bellevue military hospital in Quebec. She was surprised when a letter arrived from Texas, where Jim was training. When she opened the envelope, out fell a piece of string. "Please tie it around your finger as a reminder to write to a certain dope soon."

Beth wrote back immediately, sparking an intense, free-ranging conversation. When she asked why "a dead earnest objector" was in the army, he replied:

> I am in the Army not because I have to be, but because I must be . . . in war or in "peace," I must be where the heart of mankind is beating—and bleeding. While I refuse to increase the hemorrhage, still I must expose my own heart voluntarily to the forces of ignorance that assail the heart of mankind.

Jim's letters continued to fall through her mail slot—from New Orleans, then North Africa, then Italy, where he was attached to an artillery division that was moving on Monte Cassino. Meanwhile, Beth was swiftly initiated into the aftermath of war. At the Sainte-Anne-de-Bellevue hospital she set up an occupational therapy department for incoming war-wounded, rehabilitating limbs on machines of her own design. In her time off, she sat in her green uniform, her head wrapped in the traditional white nursing veil, and wrote letters for those who could not.

"Letters," Beth writes in her introduction to *Please Write*, "became the frail bridge that joined Jim's battlefield reality to my hospital wards and my strivings to mend the war's lacerated minds and bodies."

Jim's letters arrived with lines blacked out by censors, the original pages photographed and reduced to five-by-four-inch rectangles of shiny paper that Beth saved, so many of them ending with "Please write often, Beth."

> The ease with which I was able to "speak" to Jim in my letters—that comfort was ever present. Feeling loved, appreciated, included in the many pages I had received, I imagined that it would be with the same ease we would be able to plan our future together . . . Somehow the dreamer in me believed that two

> creative loving people who had placed so much caring in their letters would be able to find a way to meet and surmount the obstacles. Seldom did I worry about the lasting impact of the war on Jim's emotions, or even mine . . . Still, there were the old questions: Do I know the real Jim? How can Jim know the real Beth?

In 1945, when Jim finally arrived in Toronto, they tried their best to share their personal war. "Tentatively we reached into the small corners of our separate wartime journeys: small vignettes of the tastes, smells, and sounds of foxholes and hospital wards." But they were "stranded between who we had been, and who we were yet to be. Imagining a shared life was lost in the haunting, omnipresent battle memories and hospital rows of injured youth.

"We did not fall out of love," she declares. "Our love was washed aside by a torrent of wartime memories."

In 2013, when Beth was ninety-three, she travelled to Italy with her daughter. On their itinerary was Monte Cassino, a towering promontory topped with a Benedictine monastery. Twice this sixth-century monastery has been levelled—in 1349 by an earthquake and in 1944 by Allied bombs attempting to break through the German-controlled mountain passes that led to Rome. By the time Beth arrived seventy years later, the tower had been restored from the crumbling ruin Jim had described.

"As I walked, I mourned all the young lives tortured for a lifetime by their injuries and their unshakeable memories. Placing one foot after another on the thirty-nine steps rising to the basilica, the rain splashing on my umbrella, I let all my patients and my young love know that always I would remember them."

When Beth returned to Canada, she pulled out the box of yellowed letters from Jim and set about arranging them into the book she called *Please Write*. Since that wartime correspondence, both of them had married other loves, had children and grandchildren in two different countries. In the 1970s, Jim had tracked Beth down through her father's publishing company and sent her his poems—more than two hundred of them—and his four books: *Cold Comfort*, *Colder Comfort*, *Of My Grandfather and His War*, and *Uneasy Dusts*.

They picked up their correspondence then, Beth signing her letters "Forever and fondly grateful," Jim signing his "With gratitude that has been continuous." The exchange of letters finally ended in the spring of 2014, when Jim died at the age of ninety-three. Although they lived only a few hundred miles apart—Beth in Kingston, Ontario, and Jim in Columbus, Indiana—they never met again after parting in 1945.

The year after Jim died, *Please Write* was published. Beth was ninety-five. She continued writing poetry and stories culled from her life, pieces at once graceful and sad, thoughtful and sometimes hilarious. The year she became a centenarian, she gathered them into a manuscript she called *My Journey to One Hundred*. This past fall, with the help of a friend, she designed the book and had 150 copies printed to send as Christmas gifts to her family and friends.

"But I don't have a mailing address in Mexico!" I write to Beth, bereft that I can't be with her to receive my copy.

"It will be waiting for you," she replies. "And so will I."

The Third Stage

FOR AS LONG AS SHE CAN REMEMBER, BETH HAS BEEN making books.

"Before I could write or even manage scissors, I tore white writing paper into small pieces, tucked them into an envelope, and, with the rounded fingers of childhood, handed 'my book' to my editor father. Later, with blunt-nosed scissors, I built a 'book' by cutting out gaily coloured magazine pictures, and, with paste and a metal-handled brush, laid my story in rows on the inside of a dust jacket that, until then, had covered Carl Sandburg's book *Abraham Lincoln: The Prairie Years*."

My own book-making doesn't go back nearly that far, although once, on a long ocean voyage from Canada to Brazil, I did make an entire deck of miniature playing cards, each back meticulously decorated, and a box to hold them.

As a child, Beth not only made books, she wrote poetry too. "The psychologist in me is suspicious of that," she says wryly. "I don't think I was interested in poetry as much as I wanted to impress my father."

Until she was in middle school, if anyone asked, she'd say her dream was to be a poet and a storyteller. Her father, Lorne Pierce, was by then Canada's most significant books editor, an early and dedicated promoter of Canadian writers and artists, people he often brought home for lunch. Beth got to know the icons of early twentieth-century Canadian literature from her perch on the stairs and, later, from her place at the table: "the crinkled eyes and beribboned pince-nez of the laughing poet, Charles G.D. Roberts; the visual artist C.W. Jefferys, who could talk and smoke, the cigarette never leaving his bewhiskered mouth; Wilson MacDonald, a pioneering vegetarian, emptying walnuts and raisins out of his pockets and onto his salad plate," and "what romance in the costume of Bliss Carman: a wide-brimmed hat, a soft flowing tie and round pantlegs (no steamed edges for him!). I pressed my ears into the tales and wondered if someday there would be lyrical lines penned just for me!"

When she was in grade six, the students were asked to present an oral composition on a subject that inspired them. She chose her favourite poet, Bliss Carman.

"As I started to speak, my voice was confident. My eyes reflected my passion and the pleasure of sharing a corner of my own life. I read Bliss Carman's 'An Autumn Song' that begins, 'There is something in the autumn that is native to my blood.'"

She continued with "Arnold, Master of the Scud." A quiet laugh erupted when she read the line that described the schooner: "Snoring down the Bay of Fundy / With a norther on her beam." She pressed on. By the time she reached "Twelve year old, and full of Satan / As a nut is full of meat," the class was wailing with laughter. Thankfully, the bell rang just then. "I scrambled for my papers and ran for the schoolyard, each step pounding a rhythm that screamed, 'I must be queer, poetry must be queer, I must be queer, poetry must be queer.'"

Beth abandoned writing that day. She threw herself into athletics, into fencing, archery, dance, theatre. As an adult, she became the editor of a professional art therapy journal, where she finally returned to words, savouring their shapes and their shaping, but, she says, it wasn't until she retired that she realized "I was safe and could finally write."

She took her father's diaries as her first project. Her intent was to write an account of her father's impact on Canadian culture from the diaries he kept, one for every year of his adult life. He wrote not only about the mundane details of daily life but also about his evolving vision for Canadian literature. "His entries were narrative. Not the weather. Not point form, like many diaries. A story on every page." She wrote the book on the same small walnut desk where her father had kept his Remington typewriter and where she now writes on her computer. She wasn't quite finished when her husband fell ill and died. Only through poetry could she express that grief.

He waited
for the final
blaze of autumn
brushing softly
with his last breath
my fingertips.

Alone for the first time in almost fifty years, her days finally stripped of their urgency, of other people's needs, Beth's life veered imperceptibly into its third and final stage.

Following the Floating Byways

BETH CHOOSES HER WORDS CAREFULLY. I HAVE LEARNED TO pay attention, which is harder now that I am in Mexico and we have to speak along phone lines that crackle and gasp.

Today she says, "I have a sense, with my vintage, that there are things I want to do before I leave."

Leave. Not pass. Not die.

Vintage. Not advanced age.

Vintage is different from old. It suggests not only the past but the best part of the past. The term comes from the fifteenth-century French word *vendage*, meaning wine harvest, a vintage wine being one made primarily from grapes harvested during a single year—a very good year. Not only old, but of exceptional quality.

"What things do you want to do?" I ask.

I often ask Beth questions. Sometimes she answers. In general, she doesn't like to talk about herself. She'd rather write those private thoughts on paper. Still, I have slowly come to know more about her, how she thinks, what she has lived, the things she has accepted, the ways she has adapted, celebrating what remains. I know she loves to dance and still wants to, although that is mostly behind her now. And I know she loves projects, which she dives into with enthusiasm. Projects are her panacea.

I can't read anymore—for some reason I am seeing double—but

I have been listening to Lisa Hsiao Chen's novel *Activities of Daily Living*, which spins around the notion of projects. Why we humans take them on, how projects define time, leave a mark on the present that survives into a future when the present becomes the past. Projects create the increments by which we mark a life. *Look!* we say. *This is what I did last winter, last year, ten years ago.* Beth and I have been walking and talking for a year, our notebooks already bulging with what we have both come to refer to as "the book project."

"Project" comes from the Latin *projicere*, to throw forward. The Webster dictionary calls a project an "idle scheme, an impractical design," but I find that too dismissive. Embedded in the word is the notion of a start—a throw—and an intention—forward—although it doesn't imply an end. This makes a project less a search than an opening up, allowing oneself to feel that stir of curiosity, of delight. That swelling of faith when you sense something can come of a project, this thing that Chen calls "following the floating byways of life."

"What is it you want to do before you leave?" I repeat, mentally making a list of possibilities: sort the rest of Gillian's things and get her bequests safely into the hands of their recipients; complete the manuscript based on her father's diaries.

But Beth reaches beyond her to-do list.

"I'm thinking of making something with stamps," she says.

Really? Stamps? What on earth can come of stamps?

Slip-Sliding Away

I DO NOTHING. I THINK NOTHING. I DRAPE MY LISTLESS BODY over armchairs in this rented Mexican house, lay my head against the soft weave of shawls and stare out at the palms. Or I watch television, something funny, although I have difficulty following a story and most often drift into sleep. I sleep a lot: at least twelve hours at night, another two or three in the morning, and again in the afternoons. Not light naps: deep, engulfing, dreamless sleep.

Hedda the Headache will not vacate the premises. I am afraid that, like an Edward Albee house guest, she has moved into my skull for good. For bad, more like it. I swallow Tylenol until my ears ring, then stronger painkillers from my Mexican specialists, but Hedda is heartless, and a thief. She has stolen everything I value: my eyesight, my mind, my legs. Wayne will no longer allow me to walk about on my own. Every few steps, something—Hedda?—shoves me hard and I have to work not to fall on my face. I fall down the stairs twice. Once, in a grocery store, Wayne leaves me alone for a moment while he goes to look for coffee. He points me towards the cheese display, but before I get there, I collapse sideways into a tower of olive oil bottles. Young Mexicans run to me, picking me up, dusting me off—no bones broken, no bottles either, thank goodness. A flurry of arms ferries me to the cheese counter, where I lean against the cool glass until Wayne arrives, distraught.

Mexico is the perfect place to be going through all this. Strangers are compassionate; the slightest trip or blanched look and they gather around, wanting to help. Houses are built hard up against the narrow sidewalks, so that I can walk with fingers trailing along the red adobe. Wall-walking, I call it. I rarely fall, although I return home with my palms so red they look bloodied.

Already there is enough blood. The steroids have thinned my skin until the slightest touch opens a fresh wound. I carry with me everywhere a thick roll of Band-Aids, a tube of antibiotic cream, and gauze pads. A stumble against a step curls a wide strip of skin off my shin, a wound so deep it takes six weeks to stop oozing and leaves a long, thick purple scar. In the night, the friction of the sheets abrades my arms and legs. I think I'm having night sweats, but when I turn on the light, I see blood dribbling down my wrists.

Wayne hugs me gently as he passes my chair, and a rib snaps. I lean against the table during a meal and fracture the long, thin bone of one forearm.

My nails flatten and curl like pie crust. My hair is in wisps, white straw that breaks off in my fingers. On my better days I amuse myself by shopping online for wigs.

In January, I realize with a start that I see not one tree in the distance, but three. Two months later even the close-up world is a blur.

I devote Sunday afternoons to filling my pill boxes. I have a list of medications, vitamins, and painkillers for every day of the week, twenty-six pills a day, although each day differs from the next in some significant way. I fill the boxes and double-check, find a mistake, try again, and again, until finally, after four hours of exhausting effort, I have it right.

The medications have destroyed my immune system and Covid is rampant here. Even so, we cautiously end our months of isolation and invite friends for short visits outdoors. Our courtyard opens onto the street. Wayne leaves the outside door open for our guests, no more than two at a time. He arranges two chairs by the door and two chairs at the other end of the courtyard, with side tables between the chairs, set with snacks and drinks and N95 masks. I don't say much. After ten minutes, I lay my head on Wayne's shoulder and he takes me upstairs, tucking the two of us, Hedda and me, into bed.

In March, I gather my courage to cook dinner. We invite our closest, most Covid-cautious, most forgiving friends. It takes me four days to prepare the simple dishes I serve. The meal is edible, but in the end, it's the timing I can't get right. I have become a linear thinker, one thought slogging along after the other. If I am interrupted, I have to start again. And again.

In April, we return to Canada. I can't wait to see Beth. We haven't written often; in the miasma of my illness, words and sentences are set adrift. We make a plan to pick up our Wednesday visits after my post-travel isolation, but then she is exposed to Covid, then I am, and it is the end of May before, finally, we can meet.

It is not a good day for either of us, an expression that reminds me of what the vet said about our cat Kitty. When there are more bad days than good, he said, it's time to put her down. By that criterion, I should have been put down months ago.

Wayne drives me to Beth's house. She has set up chairs and the folding side tables on the front lawn under the budding maples. The grass at our feet is that impossible newborn green, brighter than the ribbon the Celtic dancers tied around one of the trunks to mark Beth's hundredth birthday.

I collapse into the nearest chair, one of those string clamshells that hugs you in. It is a cool day, although the sun is shining. Beth brings me a wide black wool shawl that I wrap over the blue shawl I'm wearing, a blue that doesn't quite match my Mexican skirt. I can see that now, although in the bedroom where I laboured to dress, they seemed perfect.

"The blues are off," I say in dismay.

"Yes," Beth says. She misses nothing.

I slump deeper in the chair as Beth dances around me, bringing a tray of cups and a pot of hot water, little date rolls, and two mandarins, a circle of skin carefully removed from the top of each so they look like miniature jack-o'-lanterns, ready to be hollowed out. Beth is wearing her lime-green skin-tight jeans and a top swirled in lime and deep purple. She flits around like a luna moth while I sink deeper into my dark cocoon.

"You're almost a hundred and two," I say, stating the obvious, which nevertheless astonishes me.

She laughs. "Ridiculous, isn't it?"

Ridiculous, yes, that she is waiting on me, a woman thirty years her junior, although today I feel twice her age.

"The number makes no sense," she goes on, settling into her chair and taking up her mandarin, reaching to put mine into my hands. "What is it supposed to mean?"

I have some idea of what it's like to be forty, fifty, sixty, even seventy; I've been to all those places. And I have a vague notion of eighty and ninety. After all, I've been hanging around older women all my life. But what good are models? I am not the seventy-two I imagined I would be, far from it. And a hundred? A hundred and two? Beth has entered *terra incognita*. There be monsters.

Beth's ongoing monster is shingles, which have plagued her for almost four years, a band of searing nerves around her midriff that she almost never mentions, although she does now, allowing me to glimpse her pain.

"That was quite a storm this week," she says with her usual understatement. A derecho—a straight-line windstorm that brings hurricane-level winds, heavy rains, and flash floods—blew through our province, downing trees and killing eleven people. Without touching herself, Beth makes a rubbing motion across her belly. "I felt the turmoil in my skin before the wind arrived."

I sit up a little straighter and try to focus my blurry vision. Who am I to complain of the tortures Hedda has visited upon me?

When I get up to leave, Beth reaches to pick maple keys from my hair—my wispy real hair. I've bought three wigs of various lengths to see me through the coming year, but I left them on their stands. Beth knows me too well for such artifice.

"The tree is having quite an orgy up there," she says, laughing and pointing up into the maple canopy, confettied with keys. Thousands festoon the lawn and lace the driveway, as if a wedding has passed through.

Beth insists on driving me home. As I climb into her car, I make a mental note to wear the silver maple keys my granddaughter made me for my birthday last year. Beth will be delighted. But by the time we turn the corner, this thought has slipped into oblivion like all the others, gathering somewhere to wait, I hope, until Hedda leaves.

The Poisoned Apple

ON THE DAY THAT BETH HOVERED AROUND MY SLUMPING SELF, I'd brought her a gift: the stamp album I kept as a child. I've carried it with me through my life, although I am no longer sure why. I have jettisoned or lost so many other things in my many moves—my great-aunt's patented breadknife from the 1930s, with a sliding gauge to cut thick slices or thin; the bracelet of uncut gemstones my mother gave me in Brazil; my childish drawings and adolescent paintings. The stamp book has survived perhaps because it is large enough not to be misplaced, or because just the sight of it fills me with the untempered exhilaration of childhood: those exotic stamps with all their possibilities, their colours, the flowers and portraits of famous people, the commemoration of inspiring, unsettling events. My entire history is in that book—not my personal history so much as a history of the times I lived through, the times that made me who I am.

I brought the stamp book to Beth's dining table, once a mosaic of threads, sticks, and stones, now heaped with hundreds, maybe thousands of stamps, sorted into green, blue, purple, red, orange, yellow, grey.

"Oh, that's what I've been waiting for!" Beth exclaimed when I handed her the album. "New mountains of colour!"

On my next visit, Beth tells me she has laid a few of the stamp pages on a tray on her back deck. She doesn't say why, but the minute I step into her back entrance, where the rest of the book is stored, the reek of mould catches me by the throat. I thought I'd aired out the book after the flood, but now I see that threads of black mould are eating through the heavy pages.

"I'll take it back!" I say, alarmed.

"No," she says, "it's fine. I'm airing out the stamps page by page."

But I insist. Black mould is a killer and Beth's body has troubles enough without this. At home, I throw out the album covers and remove a few pages of stamps to lay across the furniture on our back terrace, spraying them again and again with a fine mist of vinegar and water.

Every evening I bring in the pages, and every morning I lay them out in the sun again, spraying, spraying, waiting for the moment when there is no longer even the faintest whiff of mould, grateful for a project of my own.

The Story of Things

LEFT TO ITS OWN DEVICES, MY CONDITION CAN FELL ME IN three ways: sudden death by aneurysm; total blindness; and/or my mind lost to dementia. All are unlikely after a year of medication, but even so, these three horsewomen pursue me, bringing urgency to my days. I can't see and I've lost the mental agility to write, although since a doctor in Emergency injected an anaesthetic block for the occipital nerve that slithers up the back of my skull, Hedda the Headache has left, for the moment at least. In her absence, I've become obsessed with things.

I spend my mornings taking photographs. Yesterday it was my mother's jewellery; the day before, the vases and bric-a-brac from my father's mother; tomorrow, my great-great-grandmother's rocking chair, and on my mother's mother's side, the spoon that belonged to my great-grandmother Alice, the first of a string of Alices that includes my mother, myself, my niece, and my eldest granddaughter. I intend to slip the images into stories I'll write about these things—how they came to me, why I value them. Perhaps I'll include a suggestion as to who should be the next guardian, although I don't really care so long as the object is loved.

On Wednesday afternoons, Wayne drives me to visit Beth. Today I hand her the first manila envelope of sweet-smelling stamp pages that I have successfully sun-washed. I have many more pages to lay out on windless days—Germany, Chile, Colombia, Uruguay, Italy, Greece, the Netherlands, the UK—but even this one thin envelope is enough to light up Beth's face.

She carries the packet to her dining room table, where piles of stamps await the arrival of more "canvases"—thin plywood boards cut to her specifications by friends. Leaning against the wall is her first stamp painting, colours swirling up a narrow rectangle almost as tall as Beth.

"Are you sure you want more stamps?" I ask.

My offering feels like coals to Newcastle, but she assures me she has projects lined up to last not only through this summer but through the coming winter too. A triptych, and after that, who knows?

"My interest in colour and pattern has got me through this Covid winter, day by day," she says, touching the new pages of stamps with something like reverence.

Before I leave, I tell Beth how I've been getting through my days—by photographing the things I love, making notes on their stories. She says nothing but walks across the room and slyly pulls open the drawer of the coffee table on which our tea tray is laid.

"Look!" she says.

A large, flat manila envelope lies on top, labelled in Beth's unique penmanship: *The Story of the Coffee Table.*

I look around the room, imagining Beth taping stories to the undersides of chairs, the backs of paintings and photographs, the insides of cupboard doors, neatly labelled prizes at the end of a scavenger hunt for those who are left behind.

Wise Elder Syndrome

IT IS POURING WITH RAIN, BUT I AM PREPARED TO WALK. I'M wearing my yellow slicker with the pocket seam ripped open a bit to accommodate my bird guide; on my feet, pink rubber boots written over with the first lines of stories and poems penned by our group during a weekend writing retreat. My eyes are so clouded now I can't read my feet, but still, it gives me pleasure to walk with words.

But we don't walk. Beth picks me up and we drive back to her house, where she has laid out our usual afternoon tea of roasted nuts, grapes, mandarins, and, for me, hot water. Beside the tea tray, a small stack of books. *The Art of Stillness* is on top. I may have read it—the title seems familiar, and I feel a sudden wave of fondness at the sight of the author's name, Pico Iyer—but the steroids have wiped my brain clean of anything else.

"I have been meditating to the images," Beth says.

Something in my brain gently closes at the word "meditating." I have tried to meditate, but never with success. Yet everything else Beth says makes sense, so why not this?

She points to the second book in the stack: *Woman, Watching*, my portrait of another older woman I admired, the self-taught naturalist Louise de Kiriline Lawrence. I threw an in-person launch party for the book in early May. (Luckily, I had sent it off to the publisher just before GCA hit.) But even though the launch was held inside an enormous, newly renovated barn, Beth wasn't ready yet to expose herself to so many people. Instead, she bought a copy from our local independent bookseller, who delivered it to her door.

"Your book is part of how I carry on," Beth says. "I read five pages or so at a time—that's all. They are like stakes in the ground that I can grab on to, to move forward through these dreadful days."

It takes my sluggish brain a few moments to remember what makes these days so dreadful: Russian soldiers bombing Ukraine; Americans gunned down by a boy sniper at a Fourth of July parade; the latest Covid variant sparking a summer surge, just when we thought the pandemic was weakening.

"There is a calmness in your book that I associate with an earlier time," she says. "I mourn that time. That calm. That certainty of values."

"But weren't the Depression and the Second World War uncertain times too?"

She shakes her head vigorously. "We knew we were doing the right thing. The alternative was Hitler. No contest! I came into adulthood certain that whatever you do, you must do it while keeping in mind your values. The basic goodness of people. One's responsibility not only to oneself, one's family and friends, but to society as a whole. Whatever I did in my life, I wanted to see some change, however small. I wanted to make things better."

For the most part, our conversations swirl around the quotidian: the news, what we're reading, creating, doing. I make a point of not asking what's going on inside her, and I don't share much about my inner life with her. Early in our walking time together, she told me that people unburden themselves to her, believing in what she calls the "wise elder syndrome." The therapist in her can't help but listen, and their burden becomes hers. Even so, something in her tone makes me now say softly, "How are you feeling?"

"A bit depressed," she says. "Worried." A friend has invited her for dinner with four of their mutual, very longtime friends, but she hasn't been with a group of people, indoors, for a meal, in more than two years. "Should I go?" She shakes her head. "It doesn't feel safe."

"Test first. Take a box of tests and get everyone to test as soon as they arrive. It's the new party game, Twirl This Up Your Nose!" I say, trying to lighten the mood.

She smiles but says nothing in response, so we move on to other topics. Her evolving stamp art. A photograph of trees that she keeps on her kitchen table, bits of kaleidoscopic paper scattered on top that she stirs with her fingertips every time she passes. The shapes rearrange into random patterns that make her pause with delight. When I get up to leave, she hands me an envelope that contains a photograph of a tree and a slither of paper pieces in green and gold.

At home, I set the photograph and the paper bits on top of the dresser in the bedroom where I spend most of my days, hoping that I will remember to stir the pieces and pause, waiting for the kaleidoscope to shift.

Above Ground and Taking Nourishment

A COUPLE OF YEARS AGO, IN MEXICO, I WAS STANDING IN LINE for the breakfast buffet in a beautiful old hacienda built in the seventeenth century, abandoned after the 1910 revolution, and restored in 1933 by the famous opera tenor and movie star José Mojica as a house for his mother. By then, Mojica was the most recognizable Mexican in Hollywood, acting and singing in the first Spanish talkies. He'd host lavish parties for his Hollywood friends at the villa in San Miguel de Allende—people like Dolores del Río, John Ford, John Wayne, and Pedro Infante. Now, almost a hundred years later, Villa Santa Monica is a boutique hotel with an excellent restaurant frequented mostly by gringos.

I was moving slowly past the chilaquiles, concha bread, and sliced papaya behind a rather large, loud American woman, who enthusiastically hailed friends across the room.

"How y'all doin'?" they called back.

"I'm above ground and taking nourishment," she yelled, letting out a farty kind of laugh.

I think of this as I greet Beth, who has become alarmingly thin. Her stovepipe pants move with the breeze; her chest is concave. Eating has become a chore: If she doesn't mince her food and take sips of water as she swallows her tiny forkfuls, she will choke. She's not alone. As we humans age, our metabolism progressively slows until the gut empties at a snail's pace. By the time we've lived a century, nothing works the way it used to.

I am far from birdlike; in fact, medications have added thirty pounds to my frame. I try to limit my intake, but I still like to talk about food, and on good days I can now cook. It is a pleasure, as creative as writing and gardening. When my granddaughter calls to tell me her university food-and-gender class is studying food as legacy and asks if I have a recipe to share, I say, "Of course! I'll send you a copy of *Alice's Cookbook*. Look up 'shortbread.'"

The Alice of the cookbook is my mother. I've been making her shortbread for as long as I've been allowed to use a stove, and I hope to continue until that privilege is taken away from me. My mother came from Scottish stock; her shortbread is buttery and crisp and not too sweet, a restrained Scottish indulgence. My granddaughter bakes batch after batch, riffing on this old recipe to create her own variations: miso shortbread, shortbread with lavender and honey. When she gets a job at a Toronto bakery called Larry's Folly, she makes stacks of Alice's shortbread to sell.

Beth's cookie of choice is a gingersnap. She nibbles at one between sips of tea.

"I have always eaten more slowly than anyone I've ever known," she says. We are sitting in lawn chairs on her front walk, colourful cushions at our backs. "I've always enjoyed the leisure around meals."

When Beth was growing up, dinner was almost the only time she saw her father. Her mother prepared their meals carefully and made sure the presentation was artistic. There was always help to serve the food, so the family dined together without interruption. Each of them was required to bring something from their day to contribute to the conversation.

I tried to do something similar with my children, although someone was always jumping up for one reason or another. (Taking phone calls was discouraged, but that was a losing battle.) Still, the older they got, the more interesting the dining table discussion. One was studying music, two were painters, one was an actress, and both of us parents were writers. We spent many mealtimes comparing the arts, the relative value of interpretative versus creative arts, how the solitude needed for creation plays out against the demands to be public, the time it takes to achieve a finished piece (we book writers deeply envied the painters and the actress), and the biggest question of all, the one without an answer: how to balance a commitment to art with earning enough to survive.

My childhood dinner table was starkly silent in comparison. "Don't speak with your mouth full!" my father would interrupt when any of us started in on a story, and we'd all hush, whether we were chewing or not. This couldn't possibly have happened at every meal, but in my memory, when I did get a chance to tell a story, my sisters would jump on me. "Why are you always so *enthusiastic?*" they'd say, as if enthusiasm gave off a stink.

"Dinner was a very special time for me," Beth says. "It still is." Even after thirty years alone, she always sets the table, arranges her food appealingly on the plate, and relights the candle in the lantern, which she has brought inside now, drawing Gillian close, sharing this time with her daughter.

Today I tackled French vanilla pudding. Yesterday—two good days in a row!—I made roasted garlic and squash soup. Both are strengthening foods I learned from my mother's and great-aunt's nursing textbooks, substituting ground flaxseed and cashews, whipped to creaminess, for the eggs and dairy.

The pudding in its single-serving glass jars is still warm in my hand when I knock on Beth's door, unannounced.

"You caught me!" she exclaims, backing up into the hallway. It is one o'clock in the afternoon and she is wearing a zip-fronted dressing gown in a pretty shade of blue. Red socks and black lace-up sneakers peek out from underneath.

She has just finished her monthly Sunday call with her two nieces, one in north-central Ontario, the other in British Columbia. Friday at four is her weekly call with her artist friend Andrea. A Toronto friend is pencilled in for one o'clock on Saturday; checking in with her daughter's lifelong friend is on Sunday at four. When I'm in Mexico, we chat on Wednesdays at three. Every morning, she and her son do a check-in. Is this her secret? Not dressing well or walking tall or pasting stamps into paintings, but a steady rhythm of shared connection?

"I've been laughing so hard," she says, wiping tears from the corners of her eyes. She holds aloft the gift bag I've handed her, with its two jars of warm pudding and a Tupperware bowl of soup. "And now I need sustenance. This is perfect!"

Beth doesn't easily invite people into her life. When she opens her door to someone, she wants it to be her choice. I wonder if she has always been like this or if it is a function of age: The more years that accumulate, the more vulnerable one becomes, the more precious the independence.

But oh, I would like to see her put some meat on those beautiful bones, and so I ask if she would consider engaging a woman I know who will deliver meals to her door.

"I'm vegetarian, you know," she says, a bit crankily.

"This woman can cook anything," I say. "She'll come and visit with you before you make a decision. You can tell her what you like to eat and how much, and she'll make it, ready for the freezer, if that's what you want. Friends of mine use her and they say the food is terrific."

"Send me her number," Beth says, but I'm pretty sure she won't call, not so long as she is above ground and taking her own kind of nourishment.

The Grateful Society

ON THE DAY THAT BETH WAS BORN, HER FATHER PACED THE path from the School of Theology at Queen's University across the lawn and down the hill to Kingston General Hospital. Lorne Pierce had trained as a Methodist minister, but he also had a strong literary bent. His doctoral thesis, which he was writing that summer at Queen's, was on Dostoyevsky's influence on Western religious thinking.

After our walk, settled under the maples on her front lawn, Beth reveals a critical piece of her father's story, one that changed the course of Canadian culture.

"He was taking courses in literature and one day he asked his professor, 'What about Canadian literature? When are we going to study that?' His professor snapped back, 'There isn't any, and what there is, isn't worth a damn!' That was the kick my father needed. He spent the rest of his life proving that man wrong."

Not long after, Lorne Pierce was appointed literary adviser to Ryerson Press, a small church-run publishing house that began in 1829 as the Methodist Book Room, producing religious pamphlets and general books. The name was changed in 1919 to honour the Book Room's first editor, Egerton Ryerson. Beth's father entered the business the following year, bringing a clear vision of the necessity of providing Canadian books to Canadian readers. By 1922, he was editor of the press and had moved his wife and little girl to Toronto. For the next forty years, he fostered Canadian writers—novelists and poets, essayists and anthologists—hiring artists from the Group of Seven to design and illustrate their books, and producing textbooks for schools, bringing Canadian prose and poetry to young readers.

"My father was a great influence on me. I lived in a cultural world; I grew up with that vocabulary. And he was always saying, 'Live your own life!' and 'Paddle your own canoe!' I must have learned some form of independent thinking, independent acting from all that."

Beth's mother was Edith Chown, from a family sometimes referred to as "Kingston royalty."

"I have Chown ears," Beth says with a laugh. "Big ones. That's why I have my hair cut like this, to hide my ears."

Beth was a teenager when her mother became interested in glass-making, especially the Mallorytown Glass Works, the first Canadian "glasshouse," which began operation in 1839 in a town near the family's summer cottage.

"My mother died of cancer when she was sixty-four. She was just discovering the roots of glass-making in Canada and that interest penetrated me," says Beth. "I went on archaeological digs for glass, I visited glass-makers in the United States and England. Once I made so many stops at antique shops that it took us nine hours to drive to the cottage from Toronto," a trip that usually took no more than three. Beth inherited her mother's glass collection, but it wasn't the glass itself that was her mother's greatest bequest—it was the understanding that a woman can be many things all at the same time.

I tell Beth that I had a good mother too. Caring. A listener. Reliable.

"Reliable," Beth muses. "We all need that."

Beth's great-aunt Alice Chown was a radical pacifist and feminist who believed in women's emancipation and the abolition of war. She was the black sheep of the family, or as Beth puts it, "Aunt Alice was an eccentric."

In June 1908, Alice pulled Beth's mother out of university and insisted she travel with her to London, England, to march in a procession of thirteen thousand suffragettes from the Embankment to the Royal Albert Hall, which the feminists affectionately called a "Temple of Liberty" for the role it played in their campaign for women's rights. The parade was a spectacle of female solidarity: women carrying banners, works of art, emblems bearing the names of famous female figures and their achievements—an object lesson in female empowerment that Edith passed on to her daughter.

"Aunt Alice ripped into my life with the intensity of a summer storm and left behind corpuscles laden with social issues," Beth says. "She had a tremendous impact on me."

Beth pulls out her copy of *The Stairway*, written by her aunt in 1921, when Beth was still an infant—a book that insisted on women's right to vote, to receive higher education, to be protected by fair labour laws, and to work in environments free of harassment. *The Stairway* hums with Alice Chown's belief in the innate goodness of individuals and with her fervent hope that the book "might give individuals faith in themselves . . . I am anxious to get one thing across—that truth in the individual soul may be trusted."

When I return her aunt's book to Beth, I tell her that when my mother wanted to go back to work, she put her plan to my father, who said, "Only so long as you keep doing everything you already do at home," at which point my mother gave up the idea. I ask Beth if Jack ever objected to her picking up her career once their children were in school.

"Oh," she says with a laugh, "the Aunt Alice in me would never have stood for such a thing!"

When Beth was fourteen, she was invited to her aunt Alice's house along with Sylvia Woodsworth, a niece of J.S. Woodsworth, who the year before had helped found the CCF, the precursor to the leftist New Democratic Party of Canada.

"Sylvia and I served the tea and biscuits," Beth recalls. "It was a new world for me. Aunt Alice would invite five conservatives, five communists, and five members of the CCF. It was all so convivial! I met the Lewises there." David Lewis, the man who coined the term "parliamentary Marxism," was being groomed to run for prime minister of Britain when he was recruited to become the architect of Canada's New Democratic Party.

"I came away from those tea parties," Beth says, "believing that discussion and respect between people of opposing points of view was a possibility."

Independent thinking from her father, historical curiosity from her mother, radical feminism from her aunt Alice, and, from them all, a belief in the arts and in the power of words to build bonds and resolve conflict—these values are still evident in almost every conversation I have with Beth.

I marvel at how she has carried the best of her childhood safely through a century.

"We have to be grateful for the start we get with our parents, our kinfolk," she says with conviction. "We learn by osmosis. What I learned was to be honest with myself and who I am."

She pauses.

"If you could see the pile of letters my parents sent me all through my youthful days. They had such adoring names for us children. Wherever my father went, he sent letters, drawings in some, poems in others. And my mother—she'd been through the loss of her own mother when she was five and her father when she was twenty, and then the Spanish flu almost took her. All the things that happened in their lives, yet they were hugely grateful."

She smiles and I can almost see the child she was. "I am so fortunate. I was raised with this, so of course I joined their Grateful Society too."

The Frame in Which We Live

I HAVE KNOWN BETH IN ONLY TWO PLACES: THIS 1970S bungalow and her nineteenth-century red-brick row house in Portsmouth Village, with the Zen garden out back, its stone sculptures set on raked gravel, the house she and Jack bought as a pied-à-terre and where years ago Beth and I drank tea and she told me she was learning Celtic dancing.

Beth was ninety-three when she moved from the little red-brick house to the beige split-level bungalow where she lives now. She chose this house because it had a downstairs apartment that would accommodate her eldest son, who was going through a difficult time. *Must we always be a parent?* I remember thinking back then, regretting all that she was leaving—the beauty, the exquisite solitude, the convenience of the village—for a move to a suburb. But visiting her now, I see the benefits. No stairs. A garage. A sunny backyard. Mature, arching trees. These four walls are as perfect in their own way as the ones she left behind.

The house where I live is in a condo village by the Cataraqui River where it joins Lake Ontario. It is a tall, narrow townhouse with seven levels and forty-nine steps. The spaces are modern, interconnected, filled with light. The house I left for this one was solid in a way that only a two-hundred-year-old stone structure can be. The house before that was built in 1880; we sanded the floors to their original sheen, reglazed the windows, restored the horsehair plaster ceilings and walls. When we peeled off the wallpaper, dozens of layers, we found a poem scratched into the plaster.

I considered myself a settled person until a magazine asked me to write an article on "home" and I realized I'd lived in twenty-six places over my lifetime. The house where I was born in Winnipeg, the rental our family moved into while my parents built the house that seemed most like home to me. Two houses in Brazil, various apartments in my early adulthood, the shack my first husband and I moved into in northern Ontario, abandoning it finally for a prefab R-2000 house we won in a silent auction, then the house in Kingston where I found the letters that became *The Convict Lover.*

Just after my sixtieth birthday, my youngest sister and I returned to Brazil. We hadn't been back since our family left in 1962. When the taxi pulled up to our hotel in Campinas, we were sobbing so hard we could hardly pay the driver. In front of us was the park where we'd spent hours playing; across the street was the building where we'd lived for two years, Edifício Itatiaia, designed, we discovered, by Oscar Niemeyer, the world-famous architect of Brasília.

A week later, the hotel manager left a message for us to meet him in the lobby at three that afternoon. When we showed up, giddy with curiosity, he walked us across the park, past the guarded entrance to the Itatiaia, and up to apartment 801, our childhood home. The man who lived there was a psychologist (my sister is a clinical psychologist) and he was writing a book (I write books). He was renting the place from Celly Campello, the Brazilian pop star I'd listened to for hours as I lay on my bed at the back of the apartment. This generous man sat in his living room while my sister and I wandered the rooms. We could have done it blindfolded, so little had changed, not even the view from the back balcony, where I once saw a woman fall to her death.

Seeing the apartment sent us on a mission to find our second home in Brazil, the house at 817 Rua Silva Téles. We walked up and down the street, recognizing nothing. Finally we stopped in a little restaurant and the bartender told us the house had been torn down and was now a parking lot. We found the parking lot and spent the rest of the afternoon kicking away circles of gravel, revealing the wood parquet of the living room, the green tile of the bathroom, the white marble of the kitchen floor, the walls as visible to us as if they were still standing. We turned our backs to the parquet, the tile and marble, and looked out to the rise of houses that used to be an arroyo flanked by favelas, and beyond that, to the wild hill where I once met an untethered palomino pony that followed me home.

"My parents always chose houses that had one foot in the country, one in the city. Minnows in one direction, sidewalks in the other. One of our houses was called La Ferme."

Beth reads me another quote from May Sarton that she copied into her notebook. "There must be many women who have not demanded 'a room of their own,' who have not realized how closely bound up one's identity can be with the frame in which one lives."

"I never had a room of my own," Beth says. "But I always had a corner, a place that was mine." Now, for thirty years, she's had an entire house to frame her solitary self.

Recently, I've been fighting the feeling that Wayne and I must make a final move, because surely our townhouse with its endless stairs is not our forever house. All our friends are moving to one-floor apartments and small bungalows where they can "age in place," yet when Beth was at my stage of life, she was staking out the shape of the house on Lower Beverley Lake she would build with her husband, and she still had two more houses ahead of her.

Every year in Mexico, on our daily walks, we scan the real estate ads, then say to each other, “That boat has sailed; we’re too old.” Yet last winter, when I passed a woman outside a small adobe house chatting with a worker, pointing to swatches of colour, cream to sunflower, painted on the wall, my heart clenched with envy.

Beth and I couldn’t find a time to visit this week. I had a literary event on the other side of the province that ate up three days. In compensation, on our way out of town, Wayne and I detoured past Beth’s house so I could slip an envelope of the last of the sun-bathed stamps inside her screen door.

When we meet again, I tell her that I passed the hours of the long drive home thinking about houses, all the shapes they take through a life, pondering how to choose the right frame for these final decades. We are sitting on her back deck, which is high enough to see over the fence into the backyard next door. Her neighbours are whimsical gardeners; the yard is punctuated by soaring trees, wound with paths that delineate not only beds of ferns and flowers but collections of pottery, glass, and garden gnomes. Beth looks up at the canopy of pine, maple, and mountain ash.

“I am thinking perhaps I might almost be ready for a retirement residence,” she muses. “But how can I leave these trees?”

Not a Birthday Gift II

IN TWO WEEKS, BETH WILL TURN A HUNDRED AND TWO.

The media are full of enthusiastic stories about people—mostly women—who have reached such an age. It's still rare enough to be noteworthy, even though some 600,000 centenarians are alive in the world today. By 2050, when I am a hundred, the United Nations estimates there will be 3.7 million of us.

Beth refuses to be interviewed, refuses to be a poster girl for longevity. She has no desire to strive for 110, when she would become a "supercentenarian," or to surpass Marie-Louise Meilleur, the Québécoise who for a time, at 117, was the oldest living person in the world, or Margaret Romans, also Québécoise, who at 113 is Canada's current record-holder.

Beth refuses the hoopla and remains calmly insistent. "No gifts!"

Even so, I scan the internet for the silk camisole I hope will slip like a feather over her shingled torso.

I won't give it to her on her birthday.

I won't say happy birthday.

Perfection

IN HER MEMOIR *STILL LIFE AT EIGHTY*, ABIGAIL THOMAS WRITES that she wanted something to mark her passage into her seventh decade. "Sixty sounded so substantial, so respectably old, a milestone." She decided to get a tattoo to celebrate the occasion, and chose a salamander "because I love the way they look, and how they feel like a little puddle of mercury in the palm of your hand, and plus they are magic."

When she turned eighty, Abigail decided it was time for another tattoo. The salamander lives on her right arm, so she stretched out her left arm for the tattoo artist. Three letters, she explained. Plain black, in boxes, like Scrabble tiles: F T S, for Fuck This Shit. She could have chosen feathers or a snake, but during the first Donald Trump presidency in the United States, FTS had become her motto: "It applies to something new every day."

When the tattoo was finished, the artist was visibly upset. "Your skin is so thin," she said, pointing to the ink blurring across Abigail's arm. The tattoo artist urged her to come back if the blurriness didn't go away.

But Abigail shook her head, and as she left the tattoo parlour, she gave the young woman a big tip. "The imperfection is perfect. Because, FTS!"

Memory

YET AGAIN, I FORGET MY APPOINTED WALK WITH BETH. I CALL her to apologize.

"At least this foggy brain isn't permanent," I say, even as I wonder, *Is it?*

Instead of walking with Beth, I am playing cards with my youngest granddaughter, who is four. We are playing the Matching Game, which I grew up calling Memory. I lay the cards face down in three rows of ten and we take turns flipping over two at a time in search of a pair—two oranges, two strawberries, two slices of watermelon.

She beats me every time. Someone watching might think I'm letting this little girl win, but they'd be wrong. I am concentrating as hard as I can. Orange in the top right; orange in the middle bottom. I know this! Oops, no, I don't. Damn, where is that other orange?

Until a year and a half ago, I had the best memory of anyone I knew. I could read a page of a book at a glance, *snap!*, and remember it forever. I always knew where I'd put things. I could recall precisely who said what to whom and on what date, going back decades. I was the family calendar, library, and archive.

Not anymore. The slipperiness of my brain astonishes me. I still expect to remember who is coming for dinner, but *whoosh*, it's gone, not only the names of the guests but the making of the dinner itself. When they come to the door, there is nothing in the oven. We go to a restaurant instead, where the gap between reading the amount of a bill and paying it is a chasm my weakened mind can't cross.

Right now, none of this matters. I am concentrating on apples and oranges.

"I win again!" this sweet girl shouts, throwing her arms up in the air, then around my neck. She looks at me sadly. "Grandma, you lose."

My life until now has been all about memory: remembering ideas, snippets of conversation, bits of books I'm reading. Writing is the end product of all this scavenging, hoarding, percolating.

I think of the Norse god Odin, who in a poem from the thirteenth century names his pet ravens Hugin (Thought) and Munin (Memory).

Hugin and Munin
Fly each day
Over the spacious earth.
I fear for Hugin,
That he come not back
Yet more anxious am I for Munin

I, too, am anxious for the return of Munin, for what good is thought without memory?

The Love of Her Life

BETH'S HUSBAND, JACK, DIED ALMOST THIRTY YEARS AGO. I TRY to imagine living alone for three decades, without the love of my life.

What else should we talk about but him?

Beth and Jack met shortly after the end of the Second World War. She had just returned home to Toronto from her wartime work as an occupational therapist in Sainte-Anne-de-Bellevue. She enrolled in the University of Toronto, choosing her favourite subjects as a way to clear the war out of her system. She moved in with her parents, and at the same time her brother Bruce moved home to complete his university degree. The house was bulging. In his off-hours, Bruce would escape to go sailing around Toronto Harbour, and occasionally Beth did too. One afternoon, after a harried sail through turbulent waters in a racing-class boat, she flew into the house, bubbling with her adventure, to find Bruce and a classmate with their dates in the living room. Her dramatic tale, laced with proper sailing terms, impressed Bruce's friend, Jack.

"I knew enough to duck the boom when we were coming about and to lend my weight to either port or starboard when we were going to hike and run with the wind," Beth writes in *My Journey to One Hundred*. After the two young men pooled their resources to buy their own sailboat, Beth was often invited out with them. She and Jack grew close. By then she was working as a therapist at the

Workmen's Compensation Board Convalescent Centre in Toronto, a state-of-the-art facility. The San Francisco Rehabilitation Center invited her to come for three months to set up a similar program there. When she left Toronto, Jack was at the train station with roses. By May, she was back in Bruce and Jack's sailboat for a blissful summer at the Pierce family cottage on Lower Beverley Lake.

> One evening after making a quick change from bathing suits to dress code for dinner at Hotel Kenney, Jones Falls, I slipped into a dress that I had made, the neckline requiring that mini-cage known as a strapless bra. Looking pretty spiffy, we started out in Jack's Ford coupe. After dinner we walked up the steep limestone steps, past the locks clustered around Jones Falls. Beside the lake, Jack asked me to marry him. I inhaled the largest breath of my lifetime, preparatory to my "Yes! Yes! Yes!" when, like the setting sun beside us, my strapless bra began to descend to my waist. With one hand on that wayward confection and one arm free, I embraced the dear man who was to be my partner for the next forty-five years.

Jack and Bruce hauled their sailboat out of the water and put it up for sale. Jack, with his half of the proceeds, bought, not a diamond, but an emerald, in honour of the Irish ancestry he and Beth shared.

My engagement ring is also green—a Brazilian tourmaline the colour of a summer forest canopy, in a silver setting that Wayne designed.

In July 1994, Wayne was on a research icebreaker, one of two making a historic sea-to-sea-to-sea crossing of the North Pole. We had been a couple for six years, living together for four of those in a somewhat uncomfortably blended family of four children. I was desperate to meet his ship in Halifax, but the timing coincided with my traditional autumn week with my mother, who was suffering from Alzheimer's. My father needed his annual break, sailing with a friend on Chesapeake Bay, so I asked my sister to stand in for the night while I picked Wayne up at the Toronto airport, whisking us off to an inn halfway to my parents' house.

Wayne had witnessed a wedding on the icebreaker and had returned home with marriage on his mind. I was missing him so much that my mind had turned in the same direction. Driving to pick him up, filled with anticipation, I ignored the early signs of a respiratory infection. I had loaded a basket with treats so we would never have to leave our room. That night, as we embraced in bed, Wayne whispered, "Will you marry me?"

"Yes!" I gasped, then crawled to the window to lift up the sash, sucking at the air. We stumbled to the car and Wayne drove like a madman to the nearest hospital, where he held me close as the doctor told me I had double pneumonia complicated by asthma.

On Christmas Eve, he slipped the green tourmaline onto my finger, a ring he'd commissioned from a silversmith during a trip to Calgary the month before, a ring I have worn for thirty years.

I lie awake at night wondering how I would survive without Wayne, my partner in life and literature. We have always shared books and baseball, stories and deep conversation, but now he also cooks my meals, he counts my pills, he holds my arm when I insist on walking even though I sway dangerously. He doesn't comment on my moon face, my balding scalp, the light beard-fuzz on my cheeks; he doesn't remark on my body, which has devolved so drastically this year. He acts as though nothing has changed, when everything has. When I tell him I don't think I'll survive this, he says with a confidence I don't feel, "We'll have years and years together yet."

I always thought he would die first. He's a man, after all; the world is full of older women like Beth whose husbands have died before them. I used to be okay with that thought, admiring those older women on their own—taking tango lessons, writing all day long, eating whatever and whenever they wanted. Now I have nightmares of Wayne dying. I've come so close to the edge of that abyss that I can see it clearly, and the darkness terrifies me.

Beth's days are now her own, but she has never for a moment stopped loving Jack, never stopped thinking of him as her husband.

"I still miss him. I still talk to him," she says to me one afternoon, the same afternoon she tells me the story of the half-a-sailboat engagement ring. "He's been gone thirty years, but I still feel very much married to my husband, very much connected to him." She looks down at the emerald that has never left her finger, the stone inseparable from her flesh.

Bio-logic

WHEN ILLNESS STRIKES, NOTHING ELSE MATTERS. THIS IS A cliché until it happens, when life as you know it really does stop. For me, no more writing, no more reading. Bodily transformations as bizarre as anything Franz Kafka could dream up. I've become an unreliable friend, often unavailable, with little to talk about except my disintegrating self.

"You are too difficult for me," my rheumatologist said when I returned from Mexico last spring. She referred me to a program director in the division of rheumatology at the university teaching hospital, a compassionate and thorough woman who actually takes her eyes off her computer to listen when I speak. I am better in some ways: My spear-in-the-skull headache is gone and I've given up most of the painkillers. The tremors and swaying have lessened, but the fatigue and the night sweats, the numbness in my extremities, the brain fog, hair loss, fragile bones, and burst capillaries persist. I've been counting on getting rid of the corticosteroids to bring me back to myself, but at the end of July the inflammation marker in my blood shoots up almost as high as it was when I was diagnosed a year ago, and so my doctor stops the process of weaning me off the steroids.

My new rheumatologist recommends a new medication—a biologic, a class of drugs produced using a living system such as a plant or animal cell. Biologics are complex, made up of over twenty-five thousand atoms, compared with Aspirin, for instance, which has as few as twenty-one. I have no idea what that means, but I find it impressive. Biologics, apparently, have been used in cancer treatment for decades.

In mid-August, I get the good news that I have been approved for the biologic. The bad news is the price—roughly $8,000 a month for a year. I have no private insurance, and the provincial health system doesn't cover this treatment. I'm still trying to figure out how to raise that kind of money when I hear from the manufacturer that I qualify for their compassionate care program. The medication will be free, all $96,000 of it. I am faint with gratitude.

My first infusion is booked for the last day of August. I show up, jittery with anticipation, to a clinic empty except for a nurse who tells me the medication has not arrived. I return the following week, when the drug is finally in hand, and she settles me into a big cushioned chair beside a window that looks out over a parking lot. I have brought my computer, the only way I can read, with the text pumped up to 56 point at 200 percent, but I am too nervous to focus. I think of all my friends who've had infusion treatments for cancer—the deadening fatigue afterwards, the baldness, the vomiting. I seesaw between joy at the thought of finally getting off the steroids and terror at what fresh hell awaits.

My infusion takes twenty minutes, plus some hanging-around time to watch for side effects. There aren't any, not immediately after and not in the days that follow. In quick succession I receive appointments for the next three infusions. If all goes well, I'll be switched to weekly self-injections and given syringes to carry with me to Mexico, where this medication is not yet available. As long as I'm on the biologic, though, I will be even more prone to infection.

"Avoid broken skin, not even a scratch," my doctor warns. "No dental work, no cataract surgery." By now, the lenses in both my eyes are heavily crusted with steroid deposits; they'll have to stay like that for another year. I don't mind. The biologic is working. Within a month, the inflammation marker in my blood drops to a third of what it was in July. I'm again being steadily weaned off the corticosteroids, with no negative consequences. Another month and I'll be off the pills that I blame for my hair loss. By this time next year, there's a good chance I'll be free of both inflammation and medication. I allow myself a cautious swing towards joy.

Beth is one of my few friends who understands. She's been through it all, or I think she has. Even so, I rarely talk about my situation. I am loath to risk shifting her from friend to therapist. If I did that, would I ever get my dear friend back?

We've hardly seen each other all summer. When I'm not ill, I'm trying to meet my obligations to promote *Woman, Watching*. Beth has had a string of irritations to deal with, quite apart from the ongoing shingles—a broken rib, a touch of heatstroke, an antibiotic dose that has her small body writhing, and the fear of a new pandemic variant that is once again filling the hospitals and graveyards. Public health reminds us to remain vigilant and to do whatever we can to lessen the wave they are sure is coming. Beth and I go back to outdoor visits with masks, but as often as not I forget the few arrangements we have the courage to make.

"The treatment was without incident, as one prefers treatments to be, although I think it tired me out," I write to Beth after the second infusion. "I slept the day away and completely forgot our plan to get together."

We have telephone visits when we can, and when the new bivalent variant vaccine arrives, I email to let her know where to sign up. But I don't share with her my greatest worry:

Is this biologic the last resort? What if it stops working?

Telling Time

IN ONE OF HER BOOKS, LUCY SANTE WRITES THAT, IN NEW YORK City, tabloids measure the day, movie posters measure the week, and storefronts measure a year. The French Nobel laureate Annie Ernaux says something similar: The sensation of time passing is not inside us, she writes, but outside us, the routines of daily life hiving off our waking hours into portions ruled by the clock.

When her children had left home and her working life came to an end, Beth tells me, she felt a need for a new relationship with time—time as it existed before humans invented devices to track it. Time as duration: the way we feel it as we live it.

We talk about time standing still and time racing on, time as a river you can't step in twice. But how do we measure time without external signs? Some aboriginal cultures measure time in "sleeps"—a journey is ten sleeps, or maybe five. And women have always measured time as the lap between one menstrual period and the next. But if sleep eludes you and your womb has dried up, what then?

Beth and I are sitting on a bench looking out over the Cataraqui River. She keeps returning to the underlying thrust of our conversations. We are circling something, that's certain, but even now I'm not sure of its shape or size. Life after seventy? Growing older? Greeting death? Being human?

"We've reached the stage where we have time," Beth says, prodding.

She is speaking of retirement, a concept that came to Canada only fifty years ago, when everyone over seventy was given the Old Age Pension. Since then, the official definition of "old age" has slipped to sixty-five, but now that the baby boomer bulge is straining the system, there is talk of raising it to seventy-five. If they do that, I won't be officially old for another year or two.

We laugh at the shifting standard, but at its heart the word "retirement" carries a whiff of solitude, of separation from active life, of defeat, and this, I think, is what doesn't sit well with Beth. She pushes against the word, trying to reframe its meaning. Not retirement but re-engagement. Not working for economic survival but taking up activities that stir the soul. Not giving up but striding forward.

"Of course," she admits, "not everyone knows at an instant what they would do if they suddenly had Time."

I tell her about Tehching Hsieh, the real-life character in Lisa Hsiao Chen's novel *Activities of Daily Living*. Hsieh once said, "When life is reduced to its minimum, time emerges." He devoted his creative life to an artistic exploration of time: living in a cage for a year; punching a clock every hour on the hour for a year; living for a year tied to a woman with an eight-foot rope. Hsieh created these epic performance works in the 1970s and '80s, when he was a young man. In 1986, on his thirty-sixth birthday, he announced his Thirteen Year Plan: He would make art for the next thirteen years and would not show it publicly. At the end of the thirteen years, on the first day of the new millennium, he issued his report, in cut-out letters pasted onto a single sheet of paper: "I kept myself alive. I passed December 31st, 1999." Shortly after, he declared that he was no longer an artist.

Hsieh is now seventy-two, almost the same age I am. It occurs to me that he could have simply waited for retirement to experience a life reduced to the pure passage of time. Or contrived to go to prison, where time is meted out in bells and gongs, days and months marked by lines scratched on a wall.

I think of my oldest sister, who, after a career as a physiotherapist, seemed lost until she picked up a camera and became immersed in photography. And of Julia "Hurricane" Hawkins, who took up running when she turned a hundred, since there was no one left to compete against her in the cycling category at the US National Senior Games. And of Reizo, a ninety-five-year-old Japanese cardiologist who, every day, sits down and draws his self-portrait, as he has for twenty years.

"I have no idea where this is going," I say to Beth, meaning all of it—our conversations, our advancing lives.

"We are telling this story so people can see how it works," Beth says with certainty. "When you retire, when you are older, you have an opportunity to spring into something you have a passion for. And it's the passion, not the something—that's what keeps you going."

What We Carry with Us

BETH'S PASSIONS ARE AN ANTIDOTE TO THE UNCERTAINTIES that plague her these days.

"The indecisive nature of the pandemic is giving me an old feeling. A very old feeling." When she was barely two, her young parents whisked her away from Kingston, where she had been cosseted by a large and loving extended family, to a new city and a new house with a new caregiver—a Barnardo girl with an unfamiliar British accent. "Those early impressions are like injuries you suffer. They never go away, and at moments like this, that insecurity, that uncertainty—those are the feelings that come back."

In Beth's earliest photograph of herself, she is not quite two. Her hair is cut in what will become her signature Dutch bob; the hem of her cotton dress droops to dark leggings and lace-up shoes. She is standing at a pedestal, which might once have held a bird bath, in the middle of the family backyard. Laundry blows in the breeze beyond the fence. Cups are arranged on the pedestal and perhaps a plate of biscuits. Beth is pouring tea for invisible friends.

My first picture was taken when I was not much older. My hair is wispy curly and so blonde it looks white. I am wearing a smocked dress and standing at the edge of my grandmother's garden, a riot of flowers and vegetables all around me. In her photo, Beth is looking at the camera, a shy smile on her face; my feet are planted, my face knotted in concentration as I strain to carry a watering can almost as tall as I am.

Many decades have passed since these two photographs were taken, yet neither of us has changed much. "Here I am, a century later," Beth writes in *My Journey to One Hundred*, "and still, I pour tea for friends more often than anyone I know!"

Tea was integral to Beth's growing up. "If you wanted to talk something over, out came the teapot! If my father had authors for a visit, more teacups. If my mother planned to entertain some of her volunteer groups, more tea. After a party, when all the guests had disappeared, out would come the tea tray and, sitting around the fireplace, we would savour the evening's conversations."

What tea is to Beth, gardens are to me: my happiest place, where I sink into the comforting cycle of seed to flower to seed, my hands in the earth as satisfying as my fingers on a computer keyboard arranging letters into words, words into sentences, something I struggle now to do. Neither my mother nor my father had a green thumb, but when I was very young, my grandmother gave me a patch to plant in her garden, and when we returned from Brazil in the early sixties, my great-aunt hired me to weed her vegetables every Saturday. I kept plants on the windowsills of my university residence rooms, on the little balcony of my first apartment, in backyards and side yards of one house after another, until the gardens grew over the years from small squares and rectangles to a sprawling acreage in mid-life where I picked violets for my son's wedding cake, flowers for a friend's funeral, lush bouquets for the stages of the literary festival I founded, daily nosegays for our dinner table and bedside. In all the twenty-six places I have called home, most of my days started in my garden, often with a watering can.

How is it that Beth and I have kept these threads strong when we have lived through so much? Beth was born in the last year of the influenza epidemic that almost claimed her mother, yet it was an oddly optimistic time: The League of Nations was formed, Palestine was established, and the Group of Seven mounted their first exhibition. When she was nine, Beth legally became a "person," along with the female half of the Canadian population. But then the stock market crashed, triggering the Great Depression that ushered in the social and political upheaval that would shape her coming of age; she remembers her mother making sandwiches that she handed to hungry men knocking at the door. Her parents lived in fear of polio, diphtheria, whooping cough, measles—diseases that raged through families, killing children by the thousands.

I was born in 1949, when Beth was twenty-nine, the year she married Jack. I don't remember a peaceful time in the world. I was still in diapers when the Communist witch hunt was launched in the United States and the Cold War with the Soviet Union began. I was a toddler when the United States detonated the first hydrogen bomb; ten when the Vietnam War started and twenty-six when it ended. I was just starting high school when Martin Luther King Jr. delivered his "I Have a Dream" speech. Seven months later, President Kennedy was assassinated, then Malcolm X in 1965, Martin Luther King Jr. three years later, and, shortly after his death, Senator Robert Kennedy. I was in my last year of high school when the Stonewall riots sparked the gay rights movement. Everyone, it seemed, was taking to the streets, protesting racial segregation, the Vietnam War, and I did too, pounding on the hoods of American cars waiting in line to cross the Ambassador Bridge into Detroit. "Wake up!" we shouted. "The time is now."

There were bright spots, of course. At school, I stood in line for the vaccines that were finally eradicating childhood diseases. I was four when the structure of DNA was unlocked, and only nine when the birth control pill made child-bearing a choice, neither of which affected me at the time, although in university I joined a group that helped pregnant students find a pro-choice doctor. I had a toddler of my own when *Roe v. Wade* made abortion legal in the United States, a toddler who was a teenager before the Canadian law criminalizing abortion was struck down.

I was in my twenties and Beth was in her fifties when the FLQ took its hostages and Prime Minister Pierre Elliott Trudeau imposed the War Measures Act. I was travelling through Europe in a VW van when the oil crisis hit and the Yom Kippur War—the Fourth Arab-Israeli War—began. Violence and upheaval were everywhere we looked: Cyprus, Argentina, Cambodia, South Africa, Afghanistan, Iran, Nicaragua, even Europe, where the Red Army Faction planted bombs, kidnapped politicians, and hijacked airplanes.

Beth was in her sixties and I was in my thirties when IBM introduced the first personal computer, propelling us into the digital age, just as the first cases of AIDS were diagnosed, a disease that raged through the decade. Canada became a fully independent country with its own constitution and a Charter of Rights and Freedoms that guaranteed individual expression while making hate speech a crime. Reactor No. 4 exploded at the Chernobyl Nuclear Power Plant, spewing radioactive particles that will make the site uninhabitable by humans for twenty thousand years. The Berlin Wall fell, the

Soviet bloc disintegrated, and the Cold War, finally, came to an end. In China, student protests in Tiananmen Square grew to a million people demanding freedom of speech, which triggered martial law and the deaths of thousands of protesters.

Beth was in her seventies, my age now, and I was in my forties when Saddam Hussein and his Iraqi army invaded Kuwait, and when the United Nations Intergovernmental Panel on Climate Change first linked the rise in global temperature to human activities. The North American Free Trade Agreement came into effect, creating a free-trade zone among Canada, the United States, and Mexico, triggering the Zapatista uprising that led, seven years later, to the March of People the Colour of the Earth, tens of thousands of brown faces filling Mexico City's Zócalo, chanting, *"Tierra! Justicia! Democracia! La paz! Libertad!"*

On October 12, 1999, just a few weeks after my fiftieth birthday, the world's population reached six billion. I wasn't hiding under my desk, certain a nuclear bomb was about to drop, but I was always waiting for the next war, the next climate disaster, stockpiling canned tomatoes and peaches in the cellar, growing enough carrots, potatoes, cabbages, and squash to last at least one winter. I was in my fifties and Beth was in her eighties, living on a planet torn apart by earthquakes, mudslides, hurricanes, tropical storms, geomagnetic storms, each worse than the one before. One lone American gunman after another took random aim at people worshipping, shopping, dancing, sitting in schools, until the United States became the mass-shooting capital of the world.

We were the first generations, with our televisions, to invite into our homes images of every shooting, every war, invasion, random bombing, riot, and revolution. The names were oddly fanciful: the

Rose Revolution in Georgia, the Orange Revolution in Ukraine, the Tulip Revolution in Kyrgyzstan and Czechoslovakia's Velvet Revolution. Al Qaeda terrorists hijacked airplanes and crashed into New York's World Trade Center, and the United States rained down fury on Afghanistan and Iraq.

The Earth itself seemed to be in revolt. Hurricane Katrina killed almost 2,000 in New Orleans; an earthquake in Kashmir, Pakistan, and Afghanistan killed 80,000; Cyclone Nargis killed 133,000 in Myanmar. Amid the carnage, a few glimmers: Same-sex marriage was made legal in Canada, and the Truth and Reconciliation Commission set about documenting the shameful history of the Indian residential school system.

Just as I was about to turn sixty and Beth was on the cusp of ninety, both of us exhausted with worry and heartbreak, the stock markets crashed, ushering in the Great Recession of 2008, the most severe worldwide economic crisis since the Great Depression. On its heels, Barack Obama became the first Black president of the United States, giving us hope. That same year, the swine flu pandemic took its first human victim in the village of La Gloria, Mexico. Shortly after, an earthquake in Haiti killed up to 300,000 people and injured another 300,000. In 2013, the acquittal of the man accused of shooting Trayvon Martin, an African-American teen, spawned #BlackLivesMatter. Four years later, allegations of sexual abuse against Harvey Weinstein caused the #MeToo movement to go viral.

I was on the cusp of seventy and Beth was about to celebrate her centenary when doctors identified the first Canadian case of Covid-19—a virus infection that spread like gossip around the world. Two years later, anti-vaccination protesters drove their trucks to Ottawa and occupied the country's capital until they were forcibly removed, inspired perhaps by the mob of Donald Trump supporters who attacked the United States Capitol Building in Washington, DC, the year before.

Now Russia has invaded Ukraine yet again. Israel's prime minister says he won't rest until Hamas is obliterated; Hamas says the same of Israel. In the United States, the Supreme Court reversed *Roe v. Wade*, obliterating the constitutional right to abortion in that country. Wildfires have reduced millions of acres to cinders while climate change hurtles on, faster than any model could predict. The permafrost is thawing, the polar caps are melting, and the circulating Gulf Stream that cools the planet will stop dead, experts say, within five years. Covid-19 is winding down—maybe—after infecting 700 million people and leaving some 30 million dead. Donald Trump, the man who was impeached for his part in the violent attack on Congress, is once again president of the United States of America.

And here Beth and I stand, paused in our weekly walk, trying to make sense of it all.

"Everyone is born into a different world," Beth says.

I nod, unable to speak. What she says is true. We pass through the same history, but each of us bears our own disasters, keeps them alive in our memories and our bones. When another crisis rises to flatten us, we pause to add it to the load.

Is it any wonder that Beth retreats to her teapot, to the serenity of her Japanese bowl? Or that I, like the hummingbirds, search for sustenance in my garden?

How else to carry on?

The Boy, the Mole

THE DAYS ARE COOLING. I FEEL WINTER IN THE AIR AND SO does Beth. Neither of us greets the chill with anything like joy.

The warblers and flycatchers, even the hawks and vultures, are gone, and I, too, feel the pull of the south. Wayne and I were due to fly to Mexico on the first of November, but our landlady there has suddenly cancelled our lease, saying she has decided to stay in the house herself. Today the manufacturer of my biologic medication contacted me to say they can only give me one month's supply of self-injection syringes at a time, and they can only ship within Canada.

Wayne and I find another rental and rebook our flights for late November, uncertain if OHIP will approve my syringes by then. The only bright side is the extra month I'll have with Beth.

Through November my conversation with Beth turns to books.

Diana Athill, in *Somewhere Towards the End*, talks about how, in the latter stages of her life, she went off novels. "I no longer feel the need to ponder human relationships—particularly not love affairs—but I do still want to be fed facts, to be given material that extends the region in which my mind can wander. What refreshment to be able to take a holiday from myself in such good company."

I have not gone off novels. Perhaps I'm not old enough, but Beth has not gone off them either. And maybe that's a good thing.

Researchers at the Yale University School of Public Health found that people who read novels for at least thirty minutes a day lived, on average, nearly two years longer than non-readers, even when they controlled for gender, education, and health. The researchers suggest that the imaginative work of constructing a fictional universe in our mind helps grease our cognitive wheels.

Beth and I share the books we are reading, handing them back and forth, sometimes reading aloud to each other, often novels but sometimes non-fiction like *The Sound of a Wild Snail Eating*, and now and then folk tales and fables.

Reading quells for a bit Beth's anxiety about the oncoming winter, when Covid cases will surely spike and icy roads will not only discourage visitors but cancel her daily walks, deepening her isolation. She has never welcomed the imposed solitude of winter, but the older she gets, the more its consequences weigh on her. As an antidote, she has sunk into *The Boy, the Mole, the Fox, and the Horse*. Every morning, she opens the book at random and spends long minutes with a single passage. She tells me, "It is a warm salute to the day, like a conversation with a friend."

The Boy, the Mole speaks unabashedly to the meaning of life, and in particular to the meaning of friendship. A *Little Prince* for our times. Perhaps this book too was originally intended for children, but it is perfect for Beth and me, a story told with the forthrightness we value and the sensitivity we crave. The four characters are all parts of the same person: the curious, open-hearted boy; the mole who is enthusiastic but wants too much; the fox, wounded by life and slow to trust, but who still hopes to join in; and the wise horse, the soul that delivers the all-important message that home is not a physical place but exists wherever we love and are loved—which is why a death can feel like the roof falling in.

"It's the loss of my daughter and my pain at being over a hundred, closer to the end than the beginning, that has increased my anxiety," Beth says.

We are silent for a bit, then she picks up the book again and opens it to a random page.

When things get difficult remember who you are.
Who am I? asked the boy.
You are loved, said the horse.

"Sometimes I meditate on a passage," Beth says. "That helps."

I am gripped by a sudden desire to stay the winter, be a support, a relief for Beth. But I know in my bones that my health won't improve in the cold.

I long to stay.

I long to leave.

I long to stay.

Stay

BETH AND I ARE SITTING IN HER CAR OVERLOOKING THE Cataraqui River. This has become our favourite spot, with its vista of the far shore and the water flowing in between, stasis and movement in a single glance. A brisk wind rattles the trees, dislodging delinquent leaves. We decide, in unison, to remain in the car with the heater on for our whole visit.

"Oh no!" I shriek suddenly, recoiling from Beth. "I had dinner with the whole family on the weekend and yesterday my daughter-in-law called to say she tested positive for Covid!"

Beth and I reach for our window switches simultaneously and the glass walls slide down into their pockets, admitting the chill breeze.

How utterly thoughtless of me! My brain no longer works properly, but that's no excuse.

"I'm so sorry!" I say. "I was careful at the dinner. We made everyone test when they came through the door and wait in another room until the test showed negative. At the dinner I was nowhere near her. I sat at the other end of the table, by an open window." I can't bear the thought that I might make Beth sick. She would never survive this virus. "What should we do? Should I leave?"

"Stay," she says.

I dig in my purse and find two fresh N95 masks. I put on one and hand the other to Beth. It is getting cold in the car, despite the heater.

I pull my shawl close and lean into the back seat to get hers, wreathe her in its rainbow folds.

I touch her arm with my bare hand. She raises a gloved hand to mine, then pulls off both her leather driving gloves and cups my hand between hers. We sit like that for a long time, saying nothing, watching the ducks and geese poking at the dwindling blades of grass.

Leave

FIRST I STRING UP THE *PAPEL PICADO*, BRIGHTLY COLOURED paper flags cut with intricate designs—skeletons riding bicycles, kissing other skeletons, wearing feather boas and fancy wide-brimmed hats—then I gather the photographs for our *ofrenda*, the traditional family altar that marks the Mexican Day of the Dead. Our *ofrenda* is crowded this year: on the lower tiers my parents, Wayne's parents, a much-loved editor, our birding mentor, and on the top tier the five close friends who died this year. Not together in a car crash, although I have experienced that too. Each of these friends died separately, three of the same onrushing cancer, two of sudden brain bleeds. Beth is not among them; so far, we have both remained Covid virgins.

Wayne and I are usually in Mexico for the Day of the Dead. I should be unpacking our *ofrenda* box stored in San Miguel. Instead, I am in Kingston, kicking through a dusting of snow, scavenging flowers to make my offering to the dead.

I approach each winter with dread, not for myself but for the people I love. I feel the creeping chill and know what it foretells: the dying time. The cold northern months take their toll on the aged and the aging, as if those already on the margins take advantage of the darkness to slip away.

This isn't just my imagination. In cold climates, more people die between December and March than at any other time of year. The statisticians call this "excess winter mortality." The number of excess winter deaths fluctuates, but consistently, most of the deceased are in their later years—and the majority are women.

An *ofrenda* is spontaneously built from low tables and boxes and whatever else comes to hand, and then it is covered by a clean white cloth. Each family's *ofrenda* is unique, although the structure must have three levels, officially representing the Father, the Son, and the Holy Ghost. I prefer to think they stand for Mexico's traditional three deaths: the death that is the retreat from the world during the last stage of life; the death of the physical body, when it is laid in the earth; and the final death, which comes when no one remembers the person who is gone.

I scour the house for books to create two tiers above the dining room table—tiers of tears, for I weep as much as I laugh as I assemble the photographs, deciding who should stand next to whom. In San Miguel today, the markets will be full of *cempasúchiles*, the large Mexican marigolds that guide the souls of the dead home. Kingston gardens are frost-blackened, but I roam the streets anyway, searching protected corners for surviving bursts of gold.

I lay the limp little marigolds I've scavenged in a pattern on the table, with candles to light the way for the wandering souls, water to give them energy for their journey, a dish of salt to purify and protect against corruption as the soul moves between worlds. Souls feed on the smell of food, so I add dishes of ripe pears and grapes, bowls of chocolate. Then the personal objects: books for the writer; a black tin crow for the man who assembled the greatest gallery of artisanal pieces in Mexico; candy for Wayne's mother. On a recent trip to Toronto, I found tamales and *pan de muerto*—bread of the dead—although there were no sugar-paste skulls on which, if I had them, I would write our names in icing.

When the *ofrenda* is ready, I light the copal in its burner and waft the pungent smoke across the tiers and up towards the skylights, as if I thought this smoke path would bring my loved ones back. I don't believe in any of this. Not really. Even so, holding these people in my heart for this day fills me with a warmth that pushes aside my dark thoughts of the oncoming, death-dealing cold.

Last Breaths

BETH WAS WITH JACK WHEN HE DIED. HE WAS IN HOSPITAL SO long that she brought art to brighten the walls of his room and in the window hung crystals that spilled arcs of colour across the walls, the floor, the bed.

She heard his last breath.

Those crystals now hang in the window of her writing room. "This morning," she tells me the next time we are together, "the sun shone through the crystals, laying a beautiful rainbow on the floor. I bent down and scooped it in my hand and we had a little conversation, Jack and I."

Beth was alone with her son Bruce, too, when he breathed his last. He was unconscious, but she sang to him anyway, sang the lullaby she'd sung to him as an infant and as a little boy. "I'd sing, 'You've had a good day, this happened and that happened, and now it's time to sleep.' As he lay dying, I sang the same song, talking about all he'd done in his life, his successes, his brilliance. He died within the hour."

But she was nowhere near her daughter when Gillian died the night she returned from a winter trip to Morocco. She was only sixty-five, a recreational therapist with patients in both Kingston and Toronto. "She fell asleep," Beth says simply, "and never woke up."

On her desk, Beth keeps the Moroccan bracelet Gillian was

wearing when she took her last breath. "Near me, where I can clasp it and feel her close."

Now that I'm hopeful I might make it out of this illness alive, I don't mind thinking about the human deaths I've witnessed. The suicides of two strangers, who both jumped from tall buildings. My childless uncle, beside whom I slept in a hospital as he drew his last breath. My father, who died in the moment I turned away to phone my son in Austria to ask him to come home. Wayne's mother, a woman we looked after for three months so she could die in her own bed.

I have seen death, but even so, I have no idea what it is like to die. A punctuation mark, I suspect. A blankness, like sleep.

Beth's friends of her youth are gone, so too the family she was born into. No one else remembers her childhood home, the literary dinner parties, the Thoreau MacDonald woodblock-print cards her father sent out every Christmas. My parents and their immediate families are gone too. The last of them to depart was my mother's sister, who died a few months shy of her one hundredth birthday. Every year when I thumb through my wedding album, I notice a few more faces gone missing: three this summer—Wayne's closest friend, the husbands of two of my close friends.

I don't talk about this with Beth. Her landscape is significantly emptier than mine.

I fantasize funerals. The church. The flowers. The eulogy. The wrenching grief. I've buried my parents, my husband's parents, a child I was desperately close to when I was sixteen. I know how grief clenches the heart, empties the bowels, blackens the mind, makes the skin hurt. How unbelievably long the sickening waves can go on.

The funerals I fantasize are never mine; I'm alive and sitting in a pew. But I fantasize deathbeds too, and the deathbed is my own. What will get me in the end? The long-drawn-out dying of cancer? The sudden smack of a bus? A spasm of the heart? Yesterday, walking my month-old grandson, I met an acquaintance who, after the usual exchange of pleasantries, said flatly, "I've had some bad news." In the middle of the pandemic, she was told she has fourth-stage lung cancer, metastasized to the spine. She looks perfectly healthy, but she'll be gone within the year.

I don't think about my own death much, but dying is a different matter. I would like to die well.

And I think about the afterlife. Not my own—but for those I leave behind.

Will I go first? Or will I, like my sister, be the one who wakes in the night to hear my husband's last breath? Will Wayne stumble out of bed like our friend the rock star and fall dead in an instant, a blockage in his lungs? Will it be cancer of the stomach (like my husband's mother), of the pancreas (like my father and two friends), a massive brain bleed (like my husband's closest friend), the slow waning of congestive heart failure (like my husband's father), or a sudden heart attack (like my mother, rescued at last from dementia)?

I am a writer. I'm used to determining the plot. What confounds me about dying is that I will have no say in the end of this story.

This, I think, is the hallmark of the new stage I have entered and that Beth has been living through for thirty years: One after another, the people we love are leaving. There are deaths all through a life—car accidents that take school friends, aggressive cancers and heart attacks out of the blue that take friends in mid-life—but now, hardly a month goes by without another face erased from the sprawling class picture of my life.

This space that Beth and I are moving through may be colourful and still full of opportunity, but it is fragile, ready at any moment to be blown away by the winds of fortune or to collapse at our feet. There are many ways into this house of cards but only one exit, and the crowd is thinning.

I tell Beth what Carl Jung once said: "The afternoon of human life must also have a significance of its own, and cannot be merely a pitiful appendage to life's morning."

She nods. "This is exactly what we've been talking about."

Jean Rhys was obsessed with her end, anxious about it, imagining it when she was scarcely out of middle age. In fact, the prospect of being old filled her with such resentment and despair that she refused to talk about it and gathered a "suicide kit" against the day when life became too awful to bear.

Beth is not like Jean Rhys. She is not obsessed with her own demise, although I know she thinks about it, because occasionally she'll say something like, " . . . in the years I have left—or months," adding with a grin, "or decades."

Beth indulges my morbid perambulations for a while, but not for long.

"We should talk about something else," she says.

Sight Lines

MY BRAIN IS IMPROVING: I CAN PUT SENTENCES TOGETHER, occasionally feel the heat of two ideas sparking. But my eyesight continues to deteriorate. Grocery shopping is a nightmare. The lines of the shelves multiply into a terrifying maze that I stumble through, pressing my nose up against labels like Mrs. Magoo. I wave at any raised arm in the distance, for fear of offending a friend I cannot see. I try to flag down every car that passes, unable to recognize a taxi until it is at my side.

Beth's greatest wish right now is to get to Toronto to visit a longtime friend; my greatest wish is to drive her. If wishes were horses, as my mother would say, beggars would ride.

I can no longer read street signs, but I am learning to read colour and shape. I recognize my husband coming towards me by the thin gap of light between his slightly bowed legs. I know one friend by her hats, another who dyes her hair pink, which makes me wish everyone would choose a distinctive hair colour—magenta, chartreuse, tangerine, turquoise.

Most people, I have discovered, have a distinctive way of moving: a hitch to their step or a leaning-into-the-wind gait. The habitual stoop of the very tall. The craning upward of the somewhat short. The rushing pace of the oversubscribed. The saunter of one who is along for the ride. If I pay close attention, I can call each of them by name.

I dig out three old pairs of glasses that I juggle to make the world clearer. My solution-of-the-moment is a cumbersome arrangement of my most recent glasses with prescription sunglasses overtop. Until a century or two ago, this was the lot of the aged: living in a landscape that grows increasingly misty, gauzed over, the eyes wrapped like a mummy before the body is truly dead.

In her memoir *Giving Up the Ghost*, Hilary Mantel—famous for her Tudor trilogy, although her earlier novel *The Giant, O'Brien* is more to my taste—talks about her life of migraines and devastating endometriosis, unremitting pain that destroyed her sense of self.

> I am writing . . . to locate myself, if not within a body, then in the narrow space between one letter and the next, between the lines where the ghosts of meanings are. Spirit needs a house and it lodges where it can . . . I have been so mauled by medical procedures, so sabotaged and made over, so thin and so fat, that sometimes I feel that each morning it is necessary to write myself into being—even if the writing is aimless doodling that no one will ever read.

I take courage from her words and from all that Beth has lived through, even though, as she says, she hasn't had to endure the worst of the indignities of old age. My own seventeen months of dislocation—fat shifting, brain dulled, eyes clouded over, bones twig-like in their fragility, blood vessels that explode into starbursts under the skin as if every day were a holiday worthy of scarlet pyrotechnics—are nothing compared with Hilary Mantel's decades, yet they are enough that I understand the draw of paper and pen, the forging of words—any old words—as ballast for the slapping waves of physical uncertainty.

Until now I didn't have brain enough to write. I still don't, but I take my cue from Mantel and begin, moving my pen blindly from my thumb, which I hold firm at the outer margin of the turquoise notebook, to the black spiral at the centre, my pen racing from thumb to spiral, thumb to spiral, catching my thoughts and splashing them into the notebook, illegible markings for no one to read.

Adiós

IT IS LATE NOVEMBER. I CONTINUE WITH THE MONTHLY INFUSIONS of biologic, but I can't travel until I receive the government-supplied syringes for self-injection. My pharmacist is primed to order the medication the minute he gets the green light. I buy three small portable coolers and ice packs, get official letters from my specialists, and line up friends to bring my medication to Mexico in the event that I am not allowed a prescription for more than one month at a time. I feel dependent on this biologic: It has kept the blood markers low and allowed a slow wean off the steroids. Whatever this medication is, it seems to be working. And so we cancel yet another flight, rebook for early December, and wait.

Illness has made me self-absorbed. I can't stop thinking of all I've lost: my hair, my memory, my brain, the way it used to work, ideas flashing up, sparking off each other, priming the pump of my pen. And my energy, that boundless, bottomless sea I used to float in, reduced now to a slender vial that empties in minutes. I mourn my perpetual self—the sense I used to have that today I am the woman I was yesterday and will be tomorrow.

Beth and I don't talk about the perils of the coming winter. Instead, we take our conversational cues from what has been gained. The brush of tight curls that is pushing up under the strands of straw hair scattered over my scalp. The migrating fat that has left my thighs thin for the first time in my life. The artery that is sometimes a wriggling worm down the side of my face, sometimes a coiled throb at my temple—a word that has nothing to do with prayer but comes from the Latin "to stretch," a thin stretch of skin over the skull, the perfect site for a mortal blow—which brings me back to the place of worship, my praying worm, the seat of my mortality.

Both my forearms are a landscape of purple bruises; in eighteen months, no matter how careful I am, not a single day has passed without a fresh capillary burst that dulls slowly from fuchsia to burgundy to claret, settling finally into a shade just shy of maroon.

"A good red for me," I say to Beth, holding a bruised arm up against my cheek. We laugh. She is wearing a sweater of this exact colour, red with deep undertones of wine.

We shift quickly from the personal to the news, marvel at its cycles. Russia invading—again? The third year of the Covid pandemic is approaching; Beth was born into the third year of the previous pandemic. The principles we fought for through the sixties and seventies—the right to abortion, equal pay for women, freedom of expression, gay marriage—all on the political table again. A despot lying and cheating to hold power in the world's most powerful country? Of course! What did we expect?

We have both lived long enough to recognize the rhythms of politics and war. We could be crushed under those wheels, but we're not. We don't idealize the past or talk about recapturing much-burnished moments. We agree that memory distorts. Disfigures.

"I want to know the now," Beth says.

The syringes have arrived! My departure date is set.

"Goodbye," Beth says as we stand at her door for the last time this year. "No," she corrects herself. "Fare well."

"*Adiós*," I say, pronouncing it the Mexican way. *A díos*. Into the hands of God. Or the gods. Or the goddesses. We like that best.

If I were a praying person, I would pray that we both last until spring.

One Hundred and Three

Seventy-Three

A Christmas Story

I TELEPHONE BETH FROM MEXICO: TEN IN THE MORNING MY time, twelve for her. A compromise that accommodates both her late nights and my early rising.

She answers not with "Hello" but "Oh! The sun is glorious today!" The sun is glorious here too, on the rooftop patio of our Mexican casita. In the near distance, I can count the spires of eleven stone churches that have held the centre of this town for at least four centuries; the oldest, for five. The sun in these mountains is always shining, it seems, always glorious, which is why the weather is rarely mentioned. But sun on snow after a northern storm? That's worthy of an exclamation.

Beth is sitting in her writing room in a shaft of sunlight, the board on which her father wrote set across the arms of her chair. I can't see this, but she tells me. She is writing her annual Christmas letter.

"I just finished living a wonderful Christmas story," she says, her voice rippling with suppressed laughter. "The man who shovels my driveway for some reason ignored the walk up to my front door. I looked in my address book, but I couldn't find his number, so I called 411. Three men with his name were listed. I couldn't remember where he lives exactly, so I made note of them all. I called the first on the list. It wasn't him, but the woman who answered was so nice, I told her about my snowy sidewalk.

"'Oh, that's terrible!' she said, and I replied, 'It *is* terrible when you are a hundred and two and have to rely on others.' The woman asked where I lived and I told her. A little while later the phone rang and it was the woman, Tammy was her name.

"'I've been there with a friend!' she said. I looked out the window and the walks were all cleared of snow. I'd been working on the computer, too absorbed to hear the scrape of their shovels. We started to laugh and she ended up saying, 'Can you give me your email so we can be in touch?' We exchanged contacts and, can you believe it? She works for a transportation service!"

I imagine Beth shaking her head in wonder. "However did I land in the arms of someone who might be able to drive me to Toronto?"

A few days later, the week before Christmas, Wayne and I attend a reading of Truman Capote's "A Christmas Memory," about the friendship between seven-year-old Buddy and his distant cousin Miss Sook, a woman in her sixties. They live in a house in Alabama with a clutch of other relatives. Every year on a morning in November, Miss Sook announces, "It's fruitcake weather! Fetch our buggy. Help me find my hat." And Buddy and Miss Sook set out on their annual pilgrimage to gather windfall pecans and buy all the other ingredients necessary to bake thirty fruitcakes, her version of quid pro quo for the people in the town. It is a heartwarming, funny story, but the actors in this performance are overly sentimental and excessively reverential, missing the dark underpinnings of Capote's memories again and again. We leave the theatre downhearted, an extension of the funk I've been in since we decided that, in the absence of children and grandchildren, we'd make a break with tradition and do absolutely nothing to make a Christmas for ourselves alone in these mountains.

As we near the intersection of Calzada de la Aurora and Calzada de la Luz—Street of the Dawn and Street of Light—who should come around the corner, pushing his wheelbarrow, but Tio Gonzalo, the flower seller who last year stopped at our door every week, offering pots of roses, marigolds, camomile, minty yerba buena, depending on the season and the fiesta about to be celebrated. Flowers that helped carry me through that first winter of GCA.

When he sees us, he bursts into a grin. He spreads his arms wide, then lifts the handles of the wheelbarrow and runs towards us. A bus waits patiently as we hug each other in the middle of the street.

"You okay?" he says, peering deeply into my face.

I smile. *"Si, mas ó menos."*

He wheels his barrow full of flowers up onto the sidewalk so the bus can pass and we catch up on all the news of the town—the new mayor so crazy, making sidewalk space so expensive that no one is selling poinsettias in Plaza Civica, Candelaria might be cancelled, and on and on. Among the roses in his barrow, there is one poinsettia left. As we talk, a car stops and the driver leans out to ask how much it is.

"No puedo la venta," Tio Gonzalo calls back.

It's not for sale. My heart falls. I've been eyeing this small, bright plant that Mexicans call *nochebuena*—Christmas Eve—and which, if I transplant it into a pot big enough, will grow into a tall shrub, the kind that lined the roads of our town in Brazil, blooming lustily every Christmas.

We hug again and are about to part when Tio Gonzalo lifts the lone poinsettia from his barrow and hands it to me.

"Feliz Navidad!" he says. And suddenly, it's Christmas.

Red Lipstick

MY MEXICAN-AMERICAN FRIEND HAS INVITED ME TO THE bullfights. I'm not her only choice, and possibly not her first choice. She has been trying to gather a gang for the New Year's Eve event, but her Mexican girlfriends are with their families and none of her gringo friends wants to go. "Too full of judgment," she says. "They don't understand—it's all ritual and tradition!"

I say yes immediately. I've been to bullfights in the Camargue in France and in San Patricio–Melaque, Mexico, events that would more accurately be described as bull-teases: entertainments from which everyone, including the bull, walks away with hearts pounding but still beating.

Whenever Wayne and I pass the bullring on our strolls through town, I wonder what goes on behind its tall red gates. The posters plastered all over Centro show bejewelled matadors from Spain, Mexico City, even a young local man. Wayne declines my friend's invitation, as does everyone except me.

I am going and I'm excited. Bullfights are deeply rooted in Mexican culture, the epitome of the life-death struggle that stands front and centre in every parade and pilgrimage.

I text my friend the day before the event. "What do I wear?"

Without pause, she replies, "The reddest lipstick."

Most of my friends don't wear lipstick or, like me, barely colour their lips with gloss to bring back some semblance of youthful rosiness. But three women I love wear the reddest red: my Mexican-American writer friend, who has been going to bullfights since she was three, my Canadian bookseller friend, and Beth.

The first is in her mid-sixties, her curls the colour of Cancún sand. I've rarely seen her hair down; it's always braided loose and low, held at the nape with a clip.

My bookseller friend also has remarkable hair, a thick mane that frames her face in waves shot through with red, silver, and darker strands—the sea at sunset. Her face is fine-boned, her skin smooth, freckled like polished granite. Her eyes are small and penetrating, alive with compassion and sometimes anger—again like the sea, those swift reversals. She has just turned seventy. Even at the breakfast table at her cottage, she arrives with lips freshly reddened, the colour renewed often through the day, after eating, after swimming, before and after late-day drinks on the wind-skinned rocks.

The last time Beth and I were together, she greeted me wearing an electric-blue top, so new that tags still danced under one arm as she rose to hug me. Around her neck, a loop of petals made from shell or thinly sliced stone in colours that rainbowed from red to peach to blue.

Beth's lipstick matched the third petal down: a clear, perfect red. When I remarked on the purity of the colour, she said, "There are only four primary colours in Japanese culture: white, black, blue, and red. Red is the sun. It speaks of strength and joy."

Beth's lips have thinned and she is older than all of us by decades, but still, her lipstick is the reddest red.

A cocky whippet of a young man passes my friend and me as we move with the crowd towards the open gates of the bullring. He is dressed in gold brocade, his stockings a shocking pink.

We find seats in the first row of benches, among women dressed to the nines, their lips a fiery red. I am wearing a mask, so no one can tell that I found no red lipstick for the bullfight. Months later, at the airport, waiting to depart this hot-blooded country, I will find the perfect shade—Absolute Red—although I soften my Absolute under just a touch of Nude Beach.

The Greatest Revolution

FEBRUARY IS OVER; WINTER IS HALFWAY OUT THE DOOR.

"I am gloriously happy to see it go," Beth writes in an email. "It's all too much. My friends are having such ghastly times. This pandemic has gone on far too long for the brain to cope."

I feel safer here in Mexico, where houses are open to the fresh air and where we can meet friends on outdoor patios. Even so, I wear an N95 mask everywhere and carry extras to give to people I meet. I line up with locals to get vaccinated, aware every waking moment that the biologic, while effectively battling my disease, has suppressed my immune system even more than the steroids.

It's the uncertainty as much as the fear and isolation that is getting to us all. Beth said this at the beginning of the pandemic and it's even truer now, as we approach the third anniversary; we are being held prisoner by this wily virus. I think of Josie Cleroux, the prisoner in my book *The Convict Lover*. He served time in Kingston Penitentiary, a stone fortress where all prisoners were locked in solitary cells, not allowed to speak unless spoken to by a guard. The theory was that isolation would lead to contemplation and thus repentance. Daily routines were repeated precisely, day after day, so that time flowed uninterrupted. Prisoners would scratch lines into the stone walls of their cells to catch and hold the passing days, counting out the time left in their sentence. On the day they thought they should be released, guards would bring them their civilian clothes, allow them to dress, then laugh and say, *No, not today*. Again and again the trick was played, the prisoners not only isolated but never knowing when their incarceration would end.

I think of this cruel joke as the provincial government lowers restrictions, then lifts them, then imposes them again. The same uncertainty. The same psychological damage.

Recently, Beth tells me, she came within a hair's breadth of ending her three-year isolation. Her long-time friends Paul and David were having a party to celebrate their birthdays and Beth decided to go. But when she learned that one of the guests had just returned from overseas, she cancelled. Thrown back into isolation, she searched for yet another way to keep up her spirits.

"Every morning I place something lovely where I will see it. I pause to let that beauty seep into me. Every evening I read *The Boy, the Mole* and take one of those gentle ideas with me to sleep."

I don't have to search for gentleness. After we close our books and turn off our bedside lights, Wayne and I reach for each other, our hands joined through the night, a gesture I vow never to take for granted.

"I'm using up your stamps," she tells me the next time I call. On Easter morning, which came early this year, she put the final stamp on her latest philatelic painting: a figure as tall as a young child, arms spread wide and raised as if in triumph. She began by sketching the image, then transferred it to a large sheet of plywood she had scored into squares. Now she is "painting" the figure with stamps. "Multicoloured for the top, blue for the jeans, red for the running shoes."

"Stamp Man!" I say.

"No," she corrects me. "Stamp Person—they're non-binary. I've been working my way towards the centre of the chest, the circle becoming smaller and smaller, until this morning I chose a red stamp for the heart."

"We need something to embrace these days," Beth says the next time I call. "We no longer live in a world that is caring. We don't care about institutions or the climate. We are not on our knees before nature."

I think of the shopping bag I was handed in a consignment shop recently. Emblazoned on the bright yellow cloth was the slogan: *To Love Yourself is the Greatest Revolution.*

Really? The *greatest*? Has our self-obsession come to this?

Beth tells me that the crocuses are about to open. That the birds are courting their mates with sweet songs. That a friend has given her a beautiful length of pieced cloth as colourful as a stained glass window, which she draped down the side of her escritoire so that she sees it every time she enters her living room. That the shopping bag woven in rainbow stripes I sent her at Christmas rests in the rocking chair, another talisman of colour.

And I think: *To be alive to the world is the greatest revolution.*

Picking Up, Letting Go

THE OTHER NIGHT I WAS SITTING ON A ROOFTOP PATIO WITH A new friend who has recently moved to Mexico.

"I was a publicist," she told me. "I wanted to be an artist—a sculptor—but my parents convinced me to study something that came with a paycheque attached."

She's retired now, a slender woman with fly-away white curls, dressed in a blousy white shirt tucked into caramel shorts beaded in white swirls. It used to be that women declared their age with their clothes—shapeless dark dresses and sensible lace-up shoes that screamed a woman who no longer cared about being attractive, her years of productivity long past.

Not Beth. And not this new friend. She could be sixty or seventy or more; I find it increasingly difficult to judge the ages of the older people I meet, especially here in Mexico, where the warmth and clear air strip away ten years at least. She leans in, her voice an excited whisper, as if by speaking the words too loudly she might invite a jinx. "I'm sculpting now! Three times a week I go to an artist's studio. I never thought I had much artistic talent, but we sketch. I sketch! Then I sculpt the portrait in clay." She raises her hands and stares at them in astonishment, as if it is a miracle what they've gotten up to.

She isn't alone in picking up an abandoned passion. In a *New York Times* article titled "Old Skills, New Rewards," Melissa Kirsch tells the stories of people who are bending in later life to pick up abandoned hobbies, resuscitate dormant skills. A man in New Hampshire returned to fly-fishing in his early seventies after a half-century lapse. "The rhythm and satisfaction of casting a fly to a waiting trout actually came back quickly," he said. What he had never forgotten, and what draws him back to the water, is the Zenlike pleasure of standing in a flowing stream.

Kirsch also spoke to a Juilliard-trained musician living in San Mateo, California, who after a twenty-eight-year hiatus picked up his violin. His neuromuscular memory was still there; he could bow a note with ease, although his fingers weren't as agile as they'd once been. "I decided not to give up, but to embrace it as a beginner again!"

The experience became a metaphor for this latter chapter of his life.

"Let go," he says. "Step aside. Let it unfold."

Crucified Woman

"DELICIOUS DAYS OF SUNSHINE AND WARMTH! THE DAFFODILS are up and blooming!" Beth exclaims even before she says hello. Since I call every Wednesday at exactly three o'clock, she knows who it is before I utter a word. "We wait so long for this delicious feeling!"

Beth has been longing to go to Toronto to see Jo Aitken, her friend of fifty years, and last week she finally made it. The trip has lifted her spirits like a hot-air balloon. Beth has known Jo since the seventies, when they both were members of the Bloor Street United Church arts committee that arranged exhibitions of paintings in a large room adjacent to the nave and invited the artist to coffee hour. One Remembrance Day, Timothy Findley read from his novel *The Wars*, and the Toronto Dance Theatre choreographed an anti-war dance.

Jo was intensely interested in the work of the sculptor Almuth Lütkenhaus. In 1979, she suggested that the arts committee visit Lütkenhaus's studio with a view to selecting a piece for the Easter service. All of them were impressed by *Crucified Woman*, a sculpture intended, the artist told them, to portray the suffering of women through the powerful symbol of crucifixion.

"We chose *Crucified Woman* for the Good Friday service," Beth recalls. "It fit perfectly, because the minister, together with several churches in the neighbourhood, had chosen as their theme 'battered wives.'"

The minister was Cliff Elliott, a man with a dual interest in theology and the arts, and a deep commitment to the lively and controversial work of the arts committee at Bloor Street United. Beth had followed him from Metropolitan United and now found herself standing with him at the centre of a controversy. As worshippers arrived for the Easter service, they found, hanging in the shadow of the imposing empty cross at the front of the church, Lütkenhaus's eight-foot sculpture of a naked woman, legs slightly apart, arms outstretched.

The press coverage was apoplectic in tone. NUDE SCULPTURE GREETS CONGREGATION, shouted a headline. Angry parishioners made threats. Elliott was accused of heresy and brought before the Toronto South Presbytery. He was not dismissed, but the controversy clung to him, even though comments from the congregation ran eleven to one in favour of *Crucified Woman*.

"Many people in the church are upset about it," one woman commented in a book about the fracas around the sculpture, "but I feel peaceful and clean, or healed, less burdened. Although I'm really quite an old woman, I feel new. I wonder if that's what people mean when they say they've been born again?"

Eventually the sculpture was returned to the artist, who donated it to Emmanuel College at the University of Toronto. After several years of debate, the college finally accepted the gift. It was installed in a garden amid silver birches, junipers, and scarlet-flowering annuals.

"The exciting part for me," Beth says, "is that the sculpture has become an important gathering place for women."

Beth didn't want to risk taking the train to visit Jo. And she didn't want to impose on anyone, neither the snow-shovelling woman nor the fellow who volunteered to chauffeur her around town to do her errands during the winter months. Fortunately, some local friends who were headed for Toronto heard about her desire and offered to take her. They left Kingston in the morning and dropped Beth off at the Art Gallery of Ontario, where she took a taxi to Jo's house.

"It was just like going home. We both cried, we were so delighted that I'd been able to come. She is having a rough time, so I was very happy to be with her. We are so close that when she was going out with her first husband, she said, 'I won't marry him until you meet him.'"

It was a long day—I almost wrote "for a 103-year-old woman," but it would have been a long day for anyone, twelve hours door to door. "On the way back," Beth tells me, "we followed the lake to Kingston. It took longer, but it was such a delight to be on the highway my parents used to drive from Toronto to our family cottage. And such a delight to be travelling through the countryside after being corralled indoors all winter."

Beth is effervescent with news. Her last living child has been dealing with ill health, but the worst is behind him now. Yesterday was the anniversary of her daughter's death, and her son-in-law paid a visit. "We sat outside in the sun, and it was good for both of us."

After three years, her daughter's will is finally ready to be executed. After Gillian died, her possessions were brought to Beth's house, where they had to be sorted and shipped, an enormous undertaking and one that kept Beth's grief alive. "Some of her art collection still has to be evaluated and shipped to the beneficiaries," Beth says, "but I can see the end."

For the first time in three years, her optimism seems to rise without effort.

"Spring has sprung," she chirps into the phone. "Everything is getting better!"

The Glass-Blower's Whimsy

BETH IS FINGERING A THICK LOOP OF GLASS, A RING MADE FOR some fairy-tale finger. The colour is exquisite, that place in the rainbow where green meets blue and becomes something new and watery.

"Marine," Beth declares.

This is the first time we have seen each other since November. I've been back in Canada for two months, but either she's been sick or I have. Also, in the wake of Covid's ebbing, I've been travelling a lot, giving talks on *Woman, Watching* and its heroine, Louise de Kiriline Lawrence. And Beth has had a steady stream of visitors. "At this time of year, they drop off the 401 every few days," she says, making them sound like birds—of a very special, treasured species.

I took care this morning to wear colour: a mango skirt and the cream huipil she gave me. Beth is a vision in white: white pencil jeans, white sneakers, black T-shirt, white linen blouse. She extends the blue-green glass ring towards me.

"When glass-blowers finished a piece, there was always a knob at the bottom that had to be cut off. The glass-blower would be allowed to keep the knob and they'd make something out of it, often a ring. It was called the 'glass-blower's whimsy.'"

I slip the tropical-sea ring onto my first finger, the one permanently swollen from a brutal encounter years ago with a length of freshly split firewood.

"Where did you get this bit of whimsy?" I ask, knowing by now that Beth wouldn't have shown me the ring if a story weren't attached.

"You remember I gave my collection of Ontario glass, and some of my mother's pieces too, to the new glass exhibit in Lansdowne?"

I do remember. Canadian glass was Edith Chown Pierce's "magnificent obsession." She assembled a remarkable collection and wrote the first book on the history of glass-making in Canada. Mallorytown Glassworks, the first free-blown glassworks in Canada, was long gone before the Second World War, but at Edith's persistent urging the site was scoured for shards that proved its existence. Recently, the Mallory Coach House Museum and Archives had created a permanent exhibit to celebrate Canada's first glassworks. Beth contributed many pieces, including a reproduction water pitcher commissioned by her mother when she donated the original to the Royal Ontario Museum.

"The water jug was the most beautiful shade of blue—marine, she called it—and it had what looked like a lily pad pressed up around the bowl of the pitcher. Well, the glass-blower who made that reproduction for my mother all those years ago came to the museum opening, and he brought this for me!"

Beth holds out her hand and I place the whimsy back in her palm. I have the sense she can't bear to be parted from it for long.

"When I touched it, the most extraordinary thing happened. I saw my whole life as a series of rings, each one connected to the next, not making a whole but each following the one that went before and flowing forward into the future. I realized I was weeping, tears flowing down my cheeks." She slips on the glass ring, her eyes bright with fresh tears. "It is happening again. It happens every time I hold the ring." She looks at me as if from very far away. "It gives me such joy. Such comfort."

Mother Trees

WILDFIRES HAVE BEEN BURNING WITHOUT PAUSE ALL THROUGH the spring and early summer. Millions of acres of trees up in smoke, smoke that drifts down from the north to our town on the shores of Lake Ontario. The air is so smudged we can hardly see across the street. Americans call it Canadian smoke, as if nature has a nationality, when really, these wildfires are a scourge on us all for the climate change we have caused and that will surely do in our species.

I repeat to Beth something that Louise de Kiriline Lawrence once said to me: It was good to be old because she would not live to see the worst of the devastations that were bound to come, despite our best efforts.

"I have said the same thing," Beth says grimly. She pauses, as she always does in the face of despair, scavenging for hope. This time coming up empty.

I hate camping—sleeping on the ground, cheek by jowl with other campsites, a summer subdivision among the trees. Instead, Wayne and I have been hunting for a cottage, or a property on a pond or stream that would attract wildlife and birds. Twice we came close but backed away. "We're too old to start a building project," we said to each other. We finally gave up when Covid pushed prices beyond our reach. Then, early this spring, we remembered the five acres we had kept back when we sold our country property with its beautiful two-hundred-year-old stone house and woodlands speckled with centenary trees. Those five acres are bound by a covenant that forbids permanent structures—but a tent? We ask the neighbour who set the covenant, and who still lives across the road from the property, whether a tent would be all right. Sure, he says. You could build a platform, too. Even an outhouse.

We choose a site at the farthest back corner of the property, half a kilometre in from the end of a dead-end road, hundreds of acres of woods at our back. We clear a meandering path, nothing too straight or wide or level. We agree that we will leave as light a footprint as possible on this place. I email a picture of the tent site to Beth: two mother trees arching towards each other.

"They remind me of the two maples in front of your house," I write.

She responds almost immediately. "Trees give me hope."

We set about clearing and levelling a twenty-foot-diameter space for the sleeping tent and a ten-foot one for the dining tent. My energy is failing again, I'm not sure why; I am still injecting the biologic. Mostly I watch and encourage as Wayne pulls out small saplings and low shrubs, shovels the dry earth flat and rakes it smooth. At one point, when he pauses to lean on the shovel, I say to him, "I'm seventy-three and you're seventy-four. Are we sure we should be doing this?"

"Sure. If we can, why not?"

Our neighbour helps Wayne raise the tent, which is not the usual fabric cone but a yurt tent with low side walls and windows. It is twenty feet in diameter, twelve feet high at the centre pole. Think *Out of Africa*, not Outward Bound. For weeks we have been scouring thrift shops for rugs and wicker furniture. The three six-by-nine woollen rugs look a little lost until I cover the gaps with heavy throws to create a colourful mosaic, soft underfoot. The queen bed—an inflatable mattress on a metal frame, topped with white linens, embroidered pillow covers, and a red bed scarf—takes up a fraction of the space. Plenty of room for Wayne's walnut desk as well as my three-legged mahogany table with the collapsible top, plus two folding armchairs and a coffee table cobbled from wicker baskets turned upside down and topped with a length of wood inlaid with ivory, a village scene from some unnamed palmy place. Our clothes are stacked in baskets and rattan trunks.

The yurt tent is for writing and sleeping. A few yards away is the dining tent, with a table and chairs, a cooler, and a folding counter/cabinet for dishes. Nearby, Wayne builds an outdoor cooking and washing-up area and, far down a path in the opposite direction, a latrine behind a privacy screen he weaves from saplings and twigs.

I expect the mosquitoes, the deer flies, the ticks, the mud, the awkwardness of peeing and pooping in the woods. I do not expect the total absence of human sound except for what we make. Silence enough to hear the wind moving towards us through the trees. Birdsong echoing through the forest: towhees, thrushes, owls in the night. But the biggest surprise is the soaring canvas of the tent with its shadow play of leaves and branches in the dappling sunlight. I could lie on our bed watching it for hours—and I do.

Is this what Beth found by the lake in Delta, just a few kilometres down the road from where I lie? She was my age when she and Jack built that house. When my mother and grandmother were my age, they had only a year left to live. But then I think of my father, who died at eighty-four, his mother at ninety-four, my mother's sister just a few weeks before she turned a hundred, and I shake off the notion of what is expected, what is right, what is appropriate.

Norms do not apply to individuals. As long as it seems like a good idea, and I have the strength of mind and body to do it, I will.

Beth has taught me this.

Triptych

ON THE DOOR OF THE FRIDGE, ABOVE THE DNR DETAILS FOR paramedics, Beth has pinned cartoons drawn by her daughter-in-law's wife. Beth is unmistakable with her pewter Dutch-girl haircut, high cheekbones, and slim dancer's body. In the latest cartoon, ostensibly an early 103rd birthday card, she is dancing in a purple tutu between two high-stepping postal workers under the banner: *Breaking News! Beth Robinson Leaves her Stamp on Delta Post Office!*

Summer is fully upon us when Wayne and I take a drive over to the Delta Post Office, a low-lying red-brick rural government building that is a cookie-cutter image of the post office in the village where I grew up. But, once inside, I feel as though I have stumbled into Mexico. One wall is entirely taken up with the swirl of colour that is Beth's first major stamp project: a triptych comprising two narrow, four-foot-high side panels and a wide centre panel almost as tall as she is. How I wish she were here with us! But we are alone except for the postmistress, who is beaming, clearly thrilled with this unusual artistic addition to her workplace.

"It looks like a landscape," Wayne says, standing back. "A topography of hills and rivers and plains."

I peer closely, past the red, blue, and purple borders of Queen Elizabeth II, Eisenhower, and Churchill, to the bright flowers of

Brazil, the soccer players, and the futuristic architecture of Brasília. All the years I kept those stamps, I could never have imagined this creation so intricate that it is stealing my breath.

When I get home, I look up the definition of "creator." I often look up the meaning of words I think I know, my unending quest to pull apart the tangled hair-roots of expression.

Creator: a person who brings something into existence.

The word comes, not surprisingly, from the Indo-European word for "to grow" and from the Latin *crescere*, "to spring up, to thrive, to swell."

In this triptych I see Beth thriving, and my heart swells.

Nourished by This Rich Life

BETH IS IN A CONTEMPLATIVE MOOD, THE KIND OF SPACE THAT is the wellspring of art, where ideas tumble and smack together like pebbles in a free-flowing stream. On this summer day, our entire hour together is spent in the company of Henry Moore, her first artist-love.

When Beth was in mid-life, two Moore sculptures were installed in the city where she lived: *Archer* in front of Toronto City Hall and *Two Large Forms* at one corner of the site that was home to the Art Gallery of Ontario. Henry Moore had a special relationship with the AGO; he presented the gallery with more than nine hundred sculptures and works on paper. To house it all, in 1974 the AGO opened the Henry Moore Sculpture Centre, where Beth would spend hours gazing not only on his monumental work but also on the stones and bones that inspired him.

Recently, *Two Large Forms* was removed from outside the AGO. Beth was flabbergasted. "If I had known that would ever happen—it was unthinkable to me!—I would have walked to that corner every day and photographed it, capturing how the sculpture changed with the light, with the temperature, with whoever was climbing on it."

As a child, Moore had scrambled around the rocky shores and stony cliffs of Yorkshire, where he was born, and as a sculptor he devoted himself to stone—215 carvings using forty-one different types of stone, including ten varieties of marble. Beth responded to the same thing Moore looked for in his carving. He called it "stoniness," by which he meant "its truth to material. Its tremendous power without loss of sensitiveness."

In 1975, Beth travelled with a group from the AGO to Hoglands, Moore's property near the village of Perry Green in Hertfordshire, England. She wandered the fields dotted with Moore's pierced and hollowed monumental sculptures, met Moore, and had tea with him. Shortly after, the group visited Barbara Hepworth's Trewyn Studios in St. Ives, Cornwall. Hepworth had just died in a fire, and her assistants were grieving. Nevertheless, they showed the Canadian visitors the last sculpture they'd been working on with Hepworth—marble pillars ringed by etched, gouged, and split marble orbs. Like Moore, Hepworth was from Yorkshire; they were long-time friends and congenial professional rivals. Beth walked in awe through the Palais de Danse, a former dance hall across the street from Trewyn Studios, where, since 1960, Hepworth had created her largest works. Beth was on the brink of opening her own practice as an art therapist, and as she meandered among Hepworth's powerful abstractions, the feelings they provoked deepened her understanding of the role of emotion in creation.

The mother of triplets, Hepworth somehow, heroically, managed to combine motherhood and art. "A woman artist," she argued, "is not deprived by cooking and having children, nor by nursing children with measles (even in triplicate)—one is in fact nourished by this rich life, provided one always does some work each day; even a single half hour, so that the images grow in one's mind."

"Wait," Beth says as I rise to go. We are now stricter than ever about keeping our visits to an hour, to avoid the fatigue that plagues us both. I have overstayed today, reluctant to leave this conversation that meanders across continents, through fields of art. "I want to show you my Henry Moore."

I expect a small sculpture. My first husband was a sculptor who in his early years was enthralled by Moore, especially his works on the theme of mother and child. Most of them are portraits of nurturing, although Moore also explored the darker side of the maternal bond—the submission of the mother to the aggressive needs of the child. My husband made many pieces on the mother-and-child theme, including a life-sized piece that looked like an offspring of Henry Moore and Käthe Kollwitz—a larger-than-life *Pietà* that after several exhibitions found a final resting place deep in the woods on our property in northern Ontario. Years later, when the wind blew a forest fire towards us, firefighters arrived in a helicopter and fanned out into the forest to dig a fire line. Soon two men emerged from the bush carrying the enormous fibreglass mother and child on their shoulders. I don't know what happened to that piece, but I still have my favourite mother and child of his, a white plaster bust in sweeping, abstract lines of a woman embracing an infant, her cheek against his.

Beth's Henry Moore is a signed, undated print that hangs on the wall opposite her writing room. We make our way down the hall, past the photographs of her parents, her mother's parents, Beth and her two sons playing in front of a fireplace, and "the Robinsons"—Beth, Jack, and the children—all grown up and dressed in tuxedos and long gowns. The Henry Moore print, dedicated by Moore to Beth, presents a family in dark tones grouped around a basin on the ground, the mother holding a young child, the father looking away.

I don't know what to make of the tension between the figures, their darkness stark against their larger, shadow-white selves looming behind. I would ask Beth, but she has moved on to a remarkable portrait of her father by Wyndham Lewis, famous for his portraits of Edith Sitwell, T.S. Eliot, and Ezra Pound.

"I would like to take that portrait with me in my coffin," Beth says, wrapping her arms around herself as if to embrace her father.

She knows that won't happen. Instead, the portrait will go to Queen's University. All her art will be dispersed, the framed pieces and weighty sculptures as ephemeral in a way as her bits of stone and twig on their white squares of paper. In the meantime, the art is here, where Beth needs it to be, for she believes in what Moore said: "To be an artist is to believe in life. The soul cannot thrive in the absence of art."

Memory II

FOR THE PAST FEW MONTHS, EVERY MORNING BEFORE I GET UP, I reach for my iPhone and click on the *New York Times* Spelling Bee, forcing my brain to stitch together the circle of letters to make one word after another. At first the exercise was discouraging: I never got past the level of "Nice," which is not a word I like to use. Now I can be "Amazing" in under ten minutes. Occasionally I'm a "Genius," which makes me jump out of bed with glee.

My spirits have needed boosting. Through this past spring, I have had another broken rib, an upper respiratory infection, and three courses of antibiotics. I was down to two milligrams of corticosteroids a day until the infection boosted it back up to twenty milligrams, forcing me to start the slow wean all over again.

But today, just a little over two years since the cells in the wall of my right temporal artery magically swelled into giants, I took my last tablet. I am still injecting myself every Wednesday with the biologic that promises to reset my immune system, and my legs and feet are still buzzing as if embedded with a thousand iPhones set on vibrate. But no more steroids: I cling to that. My hair will stay on my head, my bones will strengthen, the bloody maps on my arms will fade, my brain will heal—is healing.

And this afternoon, in our daily game of Memory, I lined up more pairs than my five-year-old granddaughter.

I hug her close. "Guess what!" I exclaim softly. "Grandma wins!"

The Happiness of Getting Old

ONE EVENING, AS WAYNE AND I RETURN TO THE CITY FROM the woods, I exclaim, "Look at the moon on the horizon! It's so full and bright!"

"That's the Harvey's sign," he says kindly.

I should have known. The full moon when it rises appears to me as eight overlapping opals set in an enormous sapphire within a bright golden ring.

These changes to my body are so miraculous, so bizarre, that I can't quell the urge to talk about them. But when I mention the electrical surges in my feet, my tree-trunk right leg, my pie-crust fingernails, straw hair, and white blood cells that replicate like lazy foot soldiers uninterested in fighting infection, my middle-aged children look at me with concern and say, "Are you talking to someone about this?" (by which I assume they mean a medical specialist) or "Do you have someone to talk to?" (by which I assume they mean a psychotherapist).

I have a whole roster of specialists, and a therapist too, but it's my children I want to talk to. Quite apart from this illness, I want to talk about my aging body, as a way to mitigate some of the shock for them. This will happen, I want to say. Then this. And this. It's not just me who is getting old and achy and susceptible. This will happen to you too, maybe not exactly like this, but in some way, you can count on it.

My mother tried to tell me what it was like to be her as her memories slipped their moorings and her clever brain lost its way. I didn't want to hear it. Eventually she stopped talking. I worry that I will stop talking too.

Today I bring Tomás Martínez's *The Tango Singer* to my visit with Beth. In the novel, a student travels to Buenos Aires to search amid the political protests and riots for a tango singer. He describes a party where a woman, not the tango singer, arrives looking radiant, although as the night wears on, bags slouch under her eyes. "If I pointed this out, she'd touch them with the tips of her fingers and say, without sarcasm: 'It's the happiness of getting old.'"

I read the passage to Beth. Her skin is still impossibly smooth, especially compared with mine. Now that my moon face has subsided, it's as saggy and wrinkled as a deflated balloon.

Of course, we are all growing older from the minute we slip out of the womb, but there is a point at which we deem a person to have moved beyond older, into OLD.

No matter how well we dress or how sharp our mind, the body betrays its age. Earlobes lengthen, gums recede, teeth yellow, the signature becomes shaky, the voice hushed.

"Take care of your teeth!" Beth exclaims when I ask what bodily advice she would give to a younger woman, which, I realize with a start, is me. I take her advice to heart. I no longer dismiss crowns as dental upsell but willingly submit to Dr. Hernandez, thinking I'd rather sit wide-mouthed in his chair for an hour and a half now than ten or twenty years hence.

For years Beth and I have both struggled periodically with a hoarseness that resists diagnosis. Not being able to speak firmly at normal volume made me feel frail, even though my body at the time was strong. I took breathing lessons from a respiratory physiotherapist. I cut mucus-producing foods from my diet, and when the phlegm becomes a nuisance, I inhale a mild saline solution through my nebulizer three times a day. Sometimes it doesn't work, but sometimes it does. Recently I called the telephone company to put my plan on pause during the months I'm in Mexico, and when I gave the customer service person my age—part of that endless vetting process—he exclaimed, "Really? You don't sound half that old."

Beth and I talk about mumps and measles and chicken pox, all the usual childhood diseases. In the twenties, when she was a child, there were also diphtheria, whooping cough, tuberculosis, and polio—most of these now reduced to a historical footnote. Last night, brushing her teeth before bed, Beth thought suddenly of quinsy, an old-fashioned disease like miasma and consumption and that other bygone catch-all, "a failure to thrive." Quinsy, now known as peritonsillar abscess, is a pus-filled pocket that forms near one of the tonsils, relatively rare these days when most North American children practise dental hygiene.

Beth doesn't say if her childhood was healthy, if her young body was strong. Mine was not. I've had double-over belly aches since I was seven. Roseola. Hepatitis B. Amoebic dysentery. Annual pneumonias. Choking asthma. Recurring backaches and sciatica from a fall off the bleachers at a village baseball game.

Beth and I compare our bodily malfunctions, enjoying the game, but when the subject turns to mental health, she deftly changes the subject. "You went to Delta to visit the stamp art. Tell me about *that*."

Maybe it doesn't help to attempt to understand suffering in advance. Maybe I can't smooth the way for my children, because they know that their aging will be theirs, not mine. If my grandmother had had a pacemaker, her heart might not have stopped in her sleep. If my mother had been treated with today's Alzheimer's medications, she might have been with us a decade longer. There are vaccines now for certain kinds of cancer. Who knows what fixes will be available to my children and theirs?

Still, the belief persists in me that humans, we females at least, share common experiences: We get our period and lose our period, our skin, hair, eyes, joints drying up as if we've stumbled into a desert. We submit to yearly mammograms and gynecological exams in hopes of spotting breast and cervical cancers before it's too late. Not long ago, Beth had a small growth removed from her eyebrow. When a stitch became infected, the doctor prescribed an antibiotic, giving her the usual adult dose, failing to take into account that she is a wisp of a woman weighing less than the average eleven-year-old girl, which caused her to be beset by dizziness and raging intestines.

It's just aging, the doctors say, turning away from ailments that might be addressed. It's just aging, friends say when I talk about the consequences of this disease, which in fact seem to be reversing. But even so, just because they are expected, is the constellation of changes that come with aging and illness any less distressing and difficult to bear?

All through my life I have yearned for a handbook for what was happening to my body. I noticed physical changes at first with celebration. *I have breasts! I have pubic hair! I'm bleeding, I'm a woman now!* But the party, it seems, is over. My breasts now rest on my belly. My pubis is bare. The only blood I see is what seeps from the burst capillaries under my skin, drawing maps of otherworldly places on the backs of my hands.

The Edge of Dust

BETH AND I ARE SITTING ON WHAT WE HAVE COME TO THINK OF as our bench, the second one along the path that leads away from the parking lot, the nearest to the river; the one that faces the monument to the Irishmen who died building the Rideau Canal, a waterway that extends from Kingston to the nation's capital. At this point, where the Cataraqui River meets Lake Ontario, the river is wide and calm, with little traffic except an occasional pleasure boat.

"A thousand Irishmen died building that canal," Beth says. She was here twenty years ago when the commemorative Celtic cross was unveiled. "Malaria. Blasting accidents. Rockfalls. Drownings. They worked up to their waists in water, did you know that? Without this cross, who would remember what happened to those men two hundred years ago?"

I have brought a small bowl of peaches, sliced and tossed with vanilla yogurt, which sits between us. I tell Beth about my Zoom visit with a book club that morning. They've been reading *Woman, Watching*, and one of their comments was about the extraordinary arc of Louise de Kiriline Lawrence's life, from 1894 to 1992, from pre-electricity, pre-automobile, pre-airplane to computers and close-up photos of Mars.

"I saw the first car in Delta," Beth muses. And I realize that, of course, the arc of Beth's life is even more astonishing: 1920 to 2023, from the first pandemic to this one, from the first telephone, where every call went through an operator, to a phone that is also a book, radio, television, movie theatre, newspaper, camera, heart monitor, and more.

"I don't like it," Beth says. "I don't like it one bit, the way technology has taken over." She tells me about a friend who teaches at a community college. This summer, half the essays submitted in one of his classes were written by AI. He noted the similarities and gave all the students a failing mark—and the opportunity to rewrite the paper using their own, very real intelligence.

I commiserate. "I have to work to keep up with the technology. I can't fall more than one step behind or I'll be left in the dust."

I think of Margaret Atwood's story "Torching the Dusties," in which nursing homes are set on fire, the residents torched by young people of the #OurTurn movement, furious at older generations for "killing the planet with their greed." Atwood is in her eighties, so I can't complain that such fantasies come only from the minds of the young.

Beth looks at me sideways. The wind is picking up. Our hour together is almost over. She smiles. "I'm on the edge of the dust."

Dwindling

BETH IS A WRECK TODAY—HER WORDS, NOT MINE. WE ARE parked again in front of the Irish monument, but we have not yet left the car. Yesterday she had a full-body ultrasound, considered the least invasive way to discover anomalies in internal organs, blood vessels, and soft tissue that might explain her ongoing fatigue.

"The woman was very nice," she says softly. "Very gentle. But the procedure—it was brutal."

I can see that she means the word literally. She looks pummelled as she slumps against the car door.

"I am too sensitive for this," she says wearily. "We all are."

"Until a few years ago, I was cantering along," Beth says, once she's had a few sips of tea. "I had that wonderful energy, then shingles came along." She makes the virus sound like a stranger slinking through the night. "My father had that energy, and my brother had it too. Now I have to find a mode of living where I can still feel some physical and creative energy."

Instead of Irish dancing, she stretches every morning and walks every afternoon that the weather allows. She eats well, if sparingly, is devoted to seedless green grapes so large and sweet they feel like gumdrops in the mouth. She rarely eats sugar and neither smokes nor drinks, hasn't for years. She spaces her visitors and her phone calls. The camaraderie boosts her spirits, but it also wears her out. One visit per day is good; one every other day might be better, but she has trouble resisting the stimulation of good company.

I am careful to keep my own visits short, although sometimes, I admit, our conversation slips into the next half-hour. When her speech becomes low and shaky, I leave, wishing I could detect the signs that precede that slip in her voice.

"Dwindling energy is one of the most boring things about being old," Diana Athill wrote in *Somewhere Towards the End*. "You have to resign yourself to doing less or rather, taking more breaks than you used to."

Beth agrees with the bit about taking breaks, but we both object to the phrase "resign yourself." Is there ever a stage when we don't have to adapt to what life throws at us? For two years I haven't been able to leave the house by myself for fear of falling or collapsing from fatigue. Okay, fine, then who can I find to walk out with me? It's not much different from being nine months pregnant and making sure you're never far from a bathroom, or having a gaggle of children that never allow you a moment's rest.

Our bodies make demands. We meet them. What else is there to say?

The Heart Goes Last

"THE HEART," SAYS BETH. "WE'LL GET TO THE HEART LATER."

I settle back against our park bench. I'm at ease now with Beth's habit of burying the hard bit in the middle of a story, the way my mother would crush an Aspirin on a spoon and dip it in sugar before slipping it between my lips, gently urging me to swallow.

Beth tells me about her grandson's visit, the grandson who lived with her for a year after her husband died, going to school in Kingston. "Of all the years of my life, this was one of the very best."

Her grandson had intended to arrive in the morning and leave in the late afternoon, but he and Beth were having such a good time that he stayed for supper, then, well—the guest bed was already made up, so she invited him to stay the night. He left this morning, which explains what comes next.

"This is not one of my best days," Beth says, looking out at the river. It is the last day of August and, although the sun is warmly shining, a cool breeze is shaking its head, as if summer and fall are having an argument. We know which one will win.

"So," she says, turning to me. "My heart."

She approaches this part with reluctance. She doesn't like talking about herself at the best of times, and she really doesn't like talking about her health unless the news is good. But her heart has been beating irregularly, sometimes causing discomfort. Last week, after lifting something that was too heavy, she felt a sharp pang in her chest. Her doctor hooked her up to a Holter monitor—a kind of portable electrocardiogram machine that records the electrical activity of the heart continuously over twenty-four hours or longer, one of the simplest and fastest tests for evaluating heart issues. I had noticed the monitor when I dropped by to deliver a bowl of roasted tomato soup, but I didn't ask her about it; I don't want to think about it any more than she does. I leave for Mexico in exactly one month. I want her strong enough to last another winter.

"My heart is slow," she says, letting out the story in pulses. "Sometimes it pauses. The doctor wants to put in a pacemaker."

She screws up her face at the words.

"I said to him, Look at me! Look at your chart. One. Oh. Three. I am a hundred and three years old. I don't want a pacemaker." She stiffens. "I won't have it."

As well as the DNR order stuck to her refrigerator, Beth has a thick file on her desk marked *DO NOT RESUSCITATE.* She is ready.

But am I?

Our conversation slips sideways again. Beth tells me about her daughter's friends who recently joined her for lunch, along with her son-in-law. Beth has known one of them, Gillian's closest friend, since the children were four. *It must almost be like having your daughter at the table,* I think but don't say, thank goodness, because my next thought is, *No, nothing like that at all.*

Her son-in-law brought three of Gillian's coats to the lunch. The best friend took two and Beth kept one for herself. "It is stupendous. You'll see it the next time you visit."

Her confidence inspires in me a feeling of contentment. I like the thought of something yet undone with Beth, like a dropped glove that invites me back into her world. But when I turn to her, Beth's face is fierce.

"When my son was dying—oh, he was so young, that cancer so cruel—he said to me, 'Look up, and when you see a break in a cloud, that's me.'" She scans the sky, which today is clear blue, nothing but a thin horsetail in the high heavens, signalling a change of weather. "What a gift that was. Now, when a hole appears in a cloud, I talk to him."

She talks to her husband too, in the rainbow light cast by the crystals hanging in her writing room.

And how, I wonder, does she talk to her daughter, whose death was so sudden they never had the chance to arrange an out-of-body meeting place? The lighted candle at dusk, perhaps, although I suspect that moment is still reserved for outpourings of grief from her slowly beating heart.

Stones

"AH, STONES," BETH SAYS AS WE LOOK PAST THE IRISH MONUMENT to the Cataraqui River, flowing under the antique Strauss lift bridge that seems to sing with each passing car.

It is September, the days shortening towards the fall equinox. The leaves are slow to turn this year, but here and there we point out to each other a rim of red, a splash of gold. The days of wearing masks and setting our chairs a safe ten feet apart are behind us, we hope. I lay a bright Mexican cloth on the bench and Beth sets out teacups and a thermos of fennel tea.

"Stones!" she says again, thumping her chest with her fist and looking heavenward, as if a word for the feeling that stones inspire in her might be found there.

I wait until she reaches for her tea.

"Tell me about your stone garden," I say at last.

I may not remember exactly when I met Beth, but I'll never forget meeting her stone garden.

At the turn of the millennium, Wayne and I moved to the countryside north of Kingston, into a two-hundred-year-old stone house that had begun as a small cottage. A second storey had been added so expertly, using ancient Potsdam sandstone from the same nearby quarry, that the house seemed always to have been this tall, square edifice—a hotel or a customs building—set at the edge of Upper Oak Leaf Road. Squire Moulton built our house and his two brothers built their cottages along the same carrying road, before that part of Ontario was surveyed into rectangles bounded by concession roads. We became friends with Paul and David, the couple who lived in the closest cottage. Both were retired historians and lifelong collectors; their house was filled with period furniture, hand-carved wooden bowls, mismatched china, handmade brooms. They were gardeners too, and they'd made an Eden of their small acreage, planting trees, flowering shrubs, and sweeping perennial beds punctuated with low drystone fences that Paul laid with stones he salvaged from the foundations of tumbled barns.

Beth had met Paul in the 1950s, when he was a teenager in Delta in his last year of high school, and she was a young mother with three children spending the hot months at Windrush, the family cottage. On a rainy Monday she had bumped into Paul and asked if he'd like to join the children playing with art materials around her kitchen table. After that, Paul would often stop by. He went off to university, but their friendship was renewed decades later when Beth, stranded by a flat tire, walked to the closest house to ask to use the telephone and Paul opened the door.

A year after Beth settled in the red-brick house in Portsmouth, she made her first solo trip to Ireland.

"Jack and I had been to Ireland several times, renting a car and driving through the coastal villages, stopping wherever our hearts desired," Beth says. "On our last visit before he fell ill, we discovered the Burren."

The Burren is a two-hundred-square-mile region of County Clare in the southwest of Ireland, a vast cracked pavement of glacial limestone punctuated with cliffs and caves, fossils, eerie rock formations, and archaeological sites. Ireland is often thought of as the Emerald Isle, but in the Burren, rock shelves rise from the water to a narrow band of land that has been farmed for six thousand years, then rock continues up the hillsides like the exposed ribs of ancient skeletons. The land was long ago denuded of trees, and now the cattle nibble away at the grass that springs up in the crevices, allowing wildflowers to bloom.

"It was essential that I go alone," Beth says. Jack had just died and this had been their special place. "The land I walked through rises in steps from the sea. It's the most beautiful thing to be high up looking out over the ocean, watching a storm approaching, the curtain of rain blowing in."

Every day, Beth walked out on her own, exploring the green and rocky roads. She always wore a bright yellow coat so she could be found if she tripped and fell on the uneven pathways. In her wanderings, she discovered the tiny village of Fanore and walked down a narrow lane to the remains of three fisherfolk cottages.

For twenty-four years, from the summer Jack died until 2018—the year she turned ninety-eight and contracted shingles—Beth returned to Fanore for weeks of walking.

"Each time I came to Ireland, I would go first to the abandoned, ruined cottages to say hello. I'd hold on to the stones and talk to them, saying, 'I'm glad you are still here.' Then I'd walk up the hills to another gathering of stones that marked the place where the keepers of the sheep once lived, and I spoke to those stones too. It was a very sacred ritual, my way of honouring those people who tried to survive there."

And I think: *Her way, too, of bringing Jack close.*

After Paul completed the gardens around Oak Leaf Cottage, he turned his attention to the empty field behind the house. He dredged a pond with the help of a local backhoe genius. He and David imagined wildflowers flowing from the back gate to the pond, but the wildflowers were not interested. A local shepherd suggested sheep, and so the field was fenced and a flock of sheep installed. Then Paul and David visited the Japanese Zen garden at the Museum of Canadian History and, at about the same time, recalled their neighbour complaining of a large stone he'd like to get rid of in the middle of his cornfield. Inspired by the Japanese garden, they asked the farmer's son to drag the stone to a spot beside the pond, where it was erected as the first and largest in what would become their stone garden. Paul called the stone the "eye of the storm." The sheep loved it.

Two years later, Paul asked Beth if she would like to help with the new garden. With the stones of Fanore fresh in her mind, she sat with her sketchbook on a glacial erratic in the middle of the bare limestone alvar between the house and the pond.

"There were two tall trees in the field, side by side, and beyond them, the big stone, and the pond. In my mind's eye, I saw a path running straight from the garden gate behind the house, between the trees, to the stone. But something was needed before the trees—an invitation stone."

Paul and David had amassed a huge stone pile from which they harvested rock to build their drystone fences. Paul had already selected most of the stones for the new garden, and the backhoe genius had moved them over to the site. All but three were in place, and for these, Beth had a vision.

Slowly, the garden took shape. One great stone—which Beth called "the invitation stone" and Paul called "the guardian"—rose in the middle of the path from the rose garden as if it had always been there, standing sentinel. Two more edged close to the elms, widening the gateway to the pond; another two were positioned in the open space beyond the trees. On the far side of the pond stood Beth's "grandfather stone"—Paul's "eye of the storm." And right in the middle of the pond, a stone that on the winter solstice is serendipitously kissed by the rising sun. Over the next two summers, when Beth visited Paul and David, she'd wander the property, picking up stones of various sizes that she arranged in "nests" at the feet of the massive boulders.

Paul told me that he will always think of that garden as *Carraig na caorach*, Gaelic for Rock of the Sheep. But for Beth it is a Celtic stone garden, a bit of Ireland close to hand, no ocean to cross.

Drive, Driving, Driven

IT IS TWO YEARS SINCE I HELD THE STEERING WHEEL OF A CAR. I stopped driving on a fall day not long after my GCA diagnosis. I had paused at a stoplight to make a left; the light turned green, no cars were coming, I was pretty sure of that, so I turned, barely missing a couple who had begun to cross the street. The minute I got home, I gave Wayne my car keys.

I remember the day my mother handed over the keys of her powder-blue Valiant to my youngest sister. My mother was a decade younger than I am now, and already the ganglia of Alzheimer's were twining through her brain, pinching off vital synapses. She had driven only in the tiny village where she had lived for half a century, or on the back roads to visit the cemetery where most of her family is buried, but even so, the loss of independence hit her hard.

After I relinquished my car keys, Wayne drove me everywhere, including to Beth's house. But this summer, for reasons I don't remember, Beth has got into the habit of picking me up in her silvery grey Toyota Yaris, a hundredth-birthday present to herself.

"Sporty," I say the first time I slip into the passenger seat.

"But not a sports car," she sniffs. By the time Beth was in her forties, she and Jack had two cars, one for Jack to drive to work and one for Beth. Her first was a Morris Minor, but the one she remembers most fondly was a tangerine Karmann Ghia, a sports car made by Volkswagen. "There were very few German cars in Toronto at the time. People were always honking and waving."

"Maybe it was the colour?" I say, and Beth grins.

"Could be."

After the Karmann Ghia came the MGC, a six-cylinder coupe variation on the MGB. Beth joined a British car club in Kingston and bought leather driving gloves, plus two small folding tables and a picnic basket that matched the car, so she and Jack could join the other British sports cars on excursions into the countryside.

"It's hard to know where these itches come from," she says mildly when I ask the obvious question. "My sons were into cars. They were always tearing one apart to build another. And where we lived, we had to have two cars."

I'm not buying it. When the Canadian journalist June Callwood bought herself a red Mazda Miata for her eightieth birthday, it seemed to me like a statement. A two-seater is the antithesis of a family car. It screams independence, individuality, indulgence, an Isadora Duncan kind of dare, unwrapping her head scarf to float above the boot of her roaring sports car.

I press Beth. Why not a Volkswagen Beetle? A Datsun? A Valiant, like my mother?

"For me it was an aesthetic thing. It wasn't about going fast. I liked the unusual shapes of these cars, the long snouts. I always want something interesting to look at."

All that remains of Beth's sports cars are the two little folding tables that hold our tea things when we gather under her maple trees, but Beth still loves to drive. The Yaris may not be as peppy as the sports cars she drove until Jack died, but it gets her where she wants to go—the grocery store, visiting friends in Kingston, an occasional drive into the countryside around Delta, and, once a week, to my house.

She is always waiting at the curb at precisely the allotted time, sitting pertly on her cushion with a flowered pillow at her back. She waves me into the passenger seat, her hands gloved in leather. Her right hand resting jauntily on the automatic gearshift, she backs confidently out of my driveway and heads to her house if the weather is cool or rainy, but more often to the river.

Sometimes she brings tea in a thermos and I bring hot water. Sometimes she brings grapes and I share roasted nuts, or she offers ginger cookies and I cut up peaches. We never discuss this in advance, yet somehow we never duplicate. I drape a shawl over the bench and we set up our afternoon tea between us. I could have walked this far—the path along the river starts beside the condo village where I live, and I am walking short distances by myself now—but Beth likes to drive me and I receive it as a gift.

On this bright October day, when I call for the first time from Mexico, Beth is ebullient. "I got my driver's licence renewed! I'm so relieved. I can drive for another two years. Maybe by then I won't want to drive anymore."

I can tell there's more to this story: Beth has that twinkle in her voice.

"The woman where I got my licence was all starry-eyed. She asked me, 'You're really a hundred and three?!' She couldn't believe it. The same thing happened when I got my new Covid vaccine. All these women gathered around and wanted to take pictures with me, as if they needed to hang on to me. Imagine! I've become famous for being a hundred and three!"

She paused. "I think it's my clothes. I don't wear grandmother clothes."

I see visions of my great-aunts in small-flowered dresses that hung down to their spindly ankles, or the women in my friend's seniors' residence, dressed in wildly coloured track suits with wide tops and baggy bottoms calculated to hide sagging breasts and bums—clothes built for comfort.

"I don't think it's your clothes," I say. "Maybe to them you're an icon. An icon of possibility. It's like being pregnant and everyone wanting to touch your belly, as if the newness of that life can transform their own."

"But I've done nothing," Beth insists.

"Oh yes, you have," I say, smiling. "You've lived. You are living."

Puzzling

MANY WOMEN APPROACH THEIR SEVENTIES, AND EVEN THEIR sixties, with fear and loathing. I can only imagine what they will think of becoming centenarians. When I tell my younger friends about Beth, they respond with either *Good for her!* or *Oh my god!*, which sounds a lot like *Please god, don't ever let that happen to me.*

Why, I wonder, are we so daunted by advancing age? Among the many things I have learned from spending time with Beth is that she is simply an interesting person I enjoy being with, no different from my five-year-old granddaughter, my middle-aged sons, my later-life friends.

Yet I see smooth-skinned young women spending small fortunes on anti-wrinkle creams. The waiting rooms of cosmetic surgeons are crowded with women who can't be over fifty. I admit it is tempting. I was thrilled to see that first crease under my left eye when my moon face began to wane, but that joy changed to horror as the wrinkles multiplied, recasting my face as a road map to nowhere. Every morning and night I massage my skin, tapping with my fingertips to stimulate my natural collagen, but I'm losing faith that the skin will magically tighten. I stand in front of the bathroom mirror gently pulling towards my ears, my hairline. Maybe just a wee nip and tuck? Nexsey tape to pull back my sagging neck suddenly seems like a reasonable idea.

Mexico is my reality check. Older people are respected in this culture, even revered, but just as instructive are the gringas who come here to "get work done." I recently sat through a restaurant dinner transfixed by a woman at the next table, the skin of her face pulled so tight she could hardly open her mouth to eat. Didn't she realize that while a face may be smooth, hair brightly dyed, the body lifted and shaped with Spanx and Zumba, her mottled, rope-veined hands lifting that wineglass to her frozen mouth were a dead give-away of her true age?

When I raise the subject of cosmetic surgery, Beth refuses judgment. "We have to have something to help us carry on, to stiffen our back for the journey."

She's right, of course.

"It is important to name what helps," Beth goes on. "I give orders to myself. 'Stop!' I say when I step too far into the dark side. 'Don't go there!'"

I am still casting about for what might stiffen my spine. But maybe it's simpler than I think.

"Flickering leaf-light. Colour. Solving a puzzle." Beth gives me a winking smile. "The lift you get solving one puzzle takes you to the next. And there is always another puzzle."

Death Cleaning

THE SCORPION CARCASS IS STUCK AT A RISE IN THE FLOOR where the edge of one tile is set a fraction above the others. Wayne squashed the creature with his slipper five days ago. I felt bad about that. The three-inch scorpion was sitting calmly at the door of my writing room, waiting for a spider to happen by or perhaps looking for a way back into the wild, but I couldn't quite overcome my fear and was happy Wayne came to the rescue.

I've been watching as tiny ants heave the carcass across the tiles—three four-inch tiles in three days. It took them all of yesterday to raise one scorpion pincer up over that minuscule ledge to the next tile. The ants in this mountain city are mere specks, too small to identify, although I have decided they are pharaoh ants because I like the name and because they remind me of the herculean task of moving the stones to build the pyramids. I don't see many ants around the dead scorpion, although there may be thousands underneath, feasting on its soft underparts. I don't lift the body to find out.

Death is not something anyone wants to get too close to, which is what makes *The Gentle Art of Swedish Death Cleaning* such an interesting phenomenon. First a book, then a series on Peacock TV, *Death Cleaning* rests on twin premises: Everyone is going to die and we all have way too much stuff, none of which we can take with us when we go. Best to clean it up ourselves, the show advises, before someone else has to do it.

Basically, death cleaning is an exercise in decluttering, a concept that would mystify my grandparents' generation. When we moved into our stone house in the country, we were surprised to find no closets, only four wire hooks nailed into one wall of each bedroom. The people who lived there in the nineteenth century would have had two sets of clothes: work clothes and Sunday clothes. The work clothes were washed once a week when the Sunday clothes were put on, and the Sunday clothes were washed as seldom as possible. People bought or traded for what they needed and nothing more. In his memoir, the American poet Donald Hall recalls finding a box in his grandparents' attic after they died. The box was filled with bits of string just a few inches long; the box was labelled *String Too Short to be Saved*.

Beth has been spending these past few years death cleaning, not in preparation for her own death but as a consequence of her daughter's. Gillian's husband was too distraught to face the task, so Beth's basement is crammed with the Indigenous sculptures, paintings, and fabric pieces that Gillian collected. Beth has packaged some to be shipped to museums; others she has set out for Gillian's closest friends, who are gradually dropping by to pick up their treasures as the waves of Covid recede.

Gillian's things are in the basement, but the process of distribution is so attenuated that the art and clothing and jewellery might as well be right there in the living room, for all the weight they press down on Beth. "It's been almost four years," she says. "That's cruel. Too cruel."

Death cleaning, according to the psychologist who wrote the book, is about finding out what is important to you. But every single thing that once belonged to Gillian is important to Beth, both a comfort and a spear to the heart. She can't throw anything out; it would be like throwing out Gillian. On the other hand, she can't possibly keep it all.

Beth is clearly well into her own death cleaning too, perhaps prompted by the burden of Gillian's things.

A woman comes in once a week to help Beth go through cardboard boxes of papers—her father's, her brother's, her husband's, her own. This is the penalty for outliving everyone you love: You become the guardian of their things. "But what will happen when I go?" Beth says. "No one will know what all this is, or what they should do with it."

And so she sends boxes of her father's papers and her own wartime letters to the Queen's University Archives; her letters and notes from her days with the Toronto Dance Theatre she mails back to David Earle; her sketches and notes from the dayspring festival at the Metropolitan Church go to its archives—all the layers of her life unearthed and their bits and pieces sorted and filed where others might happen upon them and fit them into some larger mosaic of life and art. She intends to have her most personal treasures cremated with her. "They've given me life and that's enough."

It is a slow, excruciating process. As one woman on the *Death Cleaning* television series blurts out, "I asked you to declutter my house—I didn't know you were going to declutter my soul!"

Everyone approaches the "things" in their life differently. When my sister's husband died of a sudden heart attack, she had his clothes out of the closet and down to the thrift store within days. A friend whose husband died suddenly in a motorcycle accident kept his bathrobe hanging on the bedroom door for years, pausing to inhale his essence every time she passed. Judgment is out of the question: There is no right or wrong way to go about the disposal of a person's things after they are gone.

"I am haunted by the stories," Beth says.

We are talking today on the phone about worldly possessions, how objects cling to us as we move through life. She tells me about a late fall day when the temperature was sinking and the December sun was lighting up the floor. "The time had come to unwrap some small bundles in my linen cupboard. For years I had been saving my Christmas cards. Reluctant to part with their images and stories, I had wrapped the cards for a tomorrow. Now the 'tomorrow' had arrived. One by one I opened the parcels. One by one I held up the shiny rectangles. Sometimes a surprise picture or note fell to my lap." She became aware of recurring themes in the notes, voices that one by one went missing from the piles. In the end, she realized, "each card, in an individual way, reveals a deep sharing and a passion for the elusive beauty in life—all strong and colourful bridges into a shared past." How could she throw them out?

I tell her about "The Practice," an essay by Ann Patchett I read recently in *The New Yorker*. When Ann was fifty-six, her best friend's father died, leaving an apartment crammed with "marvelous, useless stuff." Ann helped her friend clear it all out, and after that, these two childless women swore a solemn oath: "We would not do this to anyone." At first, Ann considered moving to a smaller house, but she loved where she lived with her husband, so she decided to go through her closets, cupboards, and drawers as if she were leaving. A practice move.

I haven't had to practise: I've moved more times than I have fingers and toes. More than two dozen moves in seventy-three years, not counting the decade of annual migrations to Mexico, where we've lived in six different houses. At each move, we lay out the excess in the driveway in what we call a yard sale, which always ends with us giving most of it away. What nobody wants, we tote to the Salvation Army. For years afterwards, I wonder if I left that favourite silk embroidery of Asian birds in a basement somewhere or if it's hanging on the wall of a thrift store scavenger thrilled with their score.

"I don't seem to have a problem with things," Beth says. "But oh! the papers!"

I think for a moment that she means her father's copious diaries, but no, she is talking about her own sheaves of notes and fragments, the product of her writing life. I suggest she contact the Queen's Archives. Every few years they come and pick up my boxes of notes and manuscripts and letters, clearing out my storage room to make room for more.

I admit to a complicated relationship with the physical objects in my universe. We have three rocking chairs, two more than anyone needs. But how can I get rid of the chair on which my Scottish great-great-grandmother rocked in her corner by the kitchen hearth in the northern Ontario log cabin where she settled with her sons? And how can I part with the rocker my grandmother's best friend gave me when I was a teenager, this chair that her mother had brought from Scotland, presented to me as a thank-you for my years of spring-cleaning her stone farmhouse? The third rocking chair belongs to my husband, who brought it with him when we moved in together—a crazy, lopsided rocker fixed by a carpenter with a slanted workshop floor. Who can resist that kind of whimsy?

"Take a picture," my son said during the last move, when I complained as I winnowed, unwilling to give anything up. But a photograph has the same failings as memory: It is a two-dimensional trap in which the wholeness of the object is lost. I've been known to stroke the cloisonné vase my great-aunt gave me, rubbing its sides like Aladdin with his lamp, feeling the stories leach into me. I never do that with a photograph.

I don't know how much Beth has culled over the years, but her life is still all around her—in her parents' furniture, in the paintings and sculptures she chose with her husband, in the ones she acquired in the solitary years since.

"I have everything I want," Beth says, "nothing more."

Shortly after she moved into this house—only her eighth in a hundred years—Beth went through the rooms and meticulously recorded each object she valued and assigned a beneficiary, pages and pages of them.

I fantasize about being like Beth, culling my vast collection of objects and assigning beneficiaries to whatever I keep. I make several starts but abandon the project every time. Maybe I'm too young. Instead, I give things away for birthdays and Christmas. Last winter, "vintage lighter" showed up on the wish list of my adult granddaughter. Aha! I still had the sterling silver Zippo my father bought in Peru in 1959. "Vintage" refers to anything at least twenty years old; "true vintage" means more than fifty years old, and this lighter was sixty-two. I polished it up and found a photograph of my father from those *Mad Men* days, the cigarette in his hand undoubtedly lit by that very lighter. My granddaughter was thrilled. I suspect the lighter, with its perky embossed llama, was thrilled too.

This thoughtful passing on of worldly goods, their stories intact, appeals to me. But there have also been unintentional cullings in my life, wholesale strippings of my worldly possessions that I wasn't party to—lost suitcases; smoke damage from an oncoming forest fire; a fog of cement dust from a construction project gone wrong; a flood that buckled floors, swelled walls, and brought ceilings crashing down on my treasured things. In the six-week triage of keep, restore, send-to-the-dump that followed the flood, we parted with many of our material possessions, some with relief, some with grief.

But how quickly things accumulate to fill the gaps! I have helped clear out four houses: my parents', my husband's parents', my spinster aunt's, and my childless aunt and uncle's. One of my dearest memories is excavating the layers in my mother's basement storage closet and discovering the bridesmaid dress I wore to my sister's wedding, where I was paired with a much older usher whom I had a mad crush on. Handling that pink crepe fabric, I felt again all the longing of first love. What I kept, though, was the crinoline my mother bought for me in New Orleans when I was ten, which I still have, tucked in a box on my storage shelves.

I loved going through those lifetime accumulations of things, searching for clues to who these people had been, who they had hoped to be. The rich Florentine bedspread Wayne's mother brought home from Europe forty years ago, still unopened in its packaging. The boxes within boxes within empty boxes my aunt saved for some unknowable purpose; the bottle of salad dressing in her fridge, thirty years past its best-before date.

Maybe the sages are right about the stages of a life—that humans inevitably reach a point of turning inwards, when "things" cease to matter. Maybe by then we're too decrepit to clear out our treasures or send them forward to a good home.

But really, why not carry our best-loved objects with us to the end? Who knows who will treasure them by then? Or perhaps we should mimic the pharaohs and tuck them around our corpse, trusted companions in an uncertain future.

"Putting your house in order, if you can do it, is one of the most comforting activities, and the benefits of it are incalculable," Leonard Cohen said. A noted minimalist, he did not expand on this theory. I can see the benefits, but the comfort he found in the doing eludes me.

Margareta Magnusson expands on Cohen's argument in *The Gentle Art of Swedish Death Cleaning*. "Death cleaning is not just mopping up," she writes. "It's a permanent reorganization, a permanent resetting of the compass toward death."

I'm not ready for that, but I think Beth is.

Magnusson wrote the book when she was "between 80 and 100." In fact, she is fourteen years younger than Beth, almost exactly halfway in age between Beth and myself. A former fashion and advertising designer, then a painter, she has moved house seventeen times within Sweden and abroad, which is why she writes, "I should know what I am talking about when it comes to deciding what to keep and what to throw away, whether you are moving house, moving country, or moving to the Great Beyond."

She insists that death cleaning is not sad, that there is great pleasure in spending time with your beloved objects before disposing of them, whether in the trash or by passing them on to your loved ones or to strangers. Wherever they end up, they'll accumulate new stories, mean something else to the person who takes them into their life. Even so, she admits, "I have death cleaned for a lot of others, but for myself, that's hard."

For the things we absolutely cannot part with, Magnusson suggests attaching notes with instructions as to where they should go. "When my mother died, she left instructions of what to do with everything. I found that consoling, as if my mother were still there telling me what to do."

Still, I wonder whether, when we've done our death cleaning, we'll say, as May Sarton does in her book *Endgame*, "I'd stripped myself of everything that keeps me more or less alive."

Raging Bulls

LAST SUMMER, MY NEXT-DOOR NEIGHBOUR CALLED THE POLICE. "I am frightened for my life," she told them. "I am terrified. I have been for three years." She is a relatively healthy woman in her nineties; a tall, elegant woman with a lookalike daughter who has moved from California, where her husband still lives, in order to see her mother through her final years. My neighbour is well cared for, she is living where she has lived for decades, her daughter is right there with her, she has nothing to fear, and yet the terror was visible in her thin face. She was so frightened she could scarcely speak.

The end of life, as I have witnessed it, is rarely pretty.

A few years ago, I read a book called *How We Die*, an attempt to categorize and describe the most common ways a human life in the twenty-first century is likely to end: cancer, stroke, heart attack, embolism, dementia. I have lost friends to all of these. I can't resist the urge to weigh the sudden suffering of a massive stroke against a lingering cancer, the swift death of a heart attack against the wasting of dementia. I have nothing to compare with the bull that escaped a bullring in Bogotá, dashed into an elevator, and gored a man to death.

It is a pointless exercise. I won't get to choose.

I have friends who, when a life-threatening illness hit, did choose their own moment to depart, some legally through MAID (Canada's Medical Assistance in Dying), while others found their own way.

Some swore they would "jump off the perch" but in the end they didn't. I suspect I too will cling to every last minute and ignore the bull raging towards me.

Life doesn't give itself up easily. Towards the end of her days, my cat named Kitty had so many strokes she fell over every time she took a step. I had to carry her to the litter box and to her food, which she refused to eat. Her fur felt like matted straw. Her bones jutted against her skin. At night, I'd lift her onto our bed and she'd slither under the covers to press the length of her body against mine, desperate for warmth. She seemed so close to dying, so miserable. The sight of her filled me with such grief that I thought it would be a kindness to us both to nudge her towards the end. I petted her and kissed her and pressed a pillow to her face. She fought like a wildcat, finding reserves of energy to push the pillow out of my hands, the life force still strong although her body wasn't.

That cat was over twenty—more than ninety in human years. I tend to do this: calculate my age and stage in terms of cats, of birds.

Louise de Kiriline Lawrence banded a female hairy woodpecker that she monitored every month for seventeen years, the oldest recorded age for that species. Yet I've never seen a bird in the woods and said to myself, *Wow! What an old bird!* I can tell a juvenile from an adult bird: The lipstick smudge on the shoulder of a young redwing blackbird that will become its adult scarlet wing patch. Brown first-year gulls that aspire to an ivory adulthood. Younger birds may be more active and have more vibrant plumage, but birds, at least to the human eye, have been spared the equivalent of the white hair, slack, wrinkled skin, stooped back, clouded vision, and tangled mind that mark advanced age in our species. There are juveniles, subadults, and adults, but there is no category for avian elders.

Of all the telltale signs of human age, it is the terrors of the mind that frighten me most. I drink my green juice every morning and walk my daily kilometres; Beth and I nibble on nuts and seeds and berries and sip herbal teas, all the while knowing we cannot avoid the endgame; we can't even choose which one we'll be forced to play. All we can do is choose where we cast our eyes.

Today, the sky is bright, the Sierra Madre mountains lift the horizon as they have done for thousands of years, the birds in the pepper tree outside my window are singing, and my heart, nudging aside my mind, sings too.

And Counting . . .

How Long? For What? With Whom?

AS A CHILD, ALL I WANTED WAS TO GROW UP. AT FIVE, I WANTED to be eight; at ten, I couldn't wait to be thirteen; at seventeen, I pretended I was twenty-two.

For many of us, the first decades of adulthood are devoted to looking ahead: building a career, a family, a life. Decades pass and still we look forward to something better. More security. More freedom. More money to buy what we want, more time to spend however we like. But then seventy, eighty, ninety hit and suddenly the future is here. If we have the courage, we stare it in the face and find beauty there. If not, we look backwards to the pleasures of the past—or its disappointments.

The future for me is no longer a golden glow in the distance. It hangs like a haze, a mist made up of questions. How will I live until the mist hardens into a wall, or a door?

How will I die? When will I die? Will my body go the final distance, will my mind?

What is the right question to ask about a life?

For years I've had a quote pinned to the bulletin board in my writing room. It is faded now, having travelled from house to house with me, lived in shadowed corners and on walls bathed in sunlight. It comes from *The Man in the Gray Flannel Suit*, a book written by

Sloan Wilson that I don't remember reading. The 1955 novel is about the American search for purpose in a world dominated by business. On a deeper level, it is about how to travel through a life.

The quote moves me as much as it did in 1987, when I was half the age I am now, printing it out and folding the paper into a square to keep always within sight:

> The main thing is to stop seeing life as a ladder, in which success depends on climbing ever higher. That's a child's dream. Life is a walk over the planet, across swamps and mountains, and the way you keep going is you just keep walking.

This reminds me of a story Subcomandante Marcos told his soldiers in the mountains of Chiapas during the Zapatista uprising. The tale is about the old gods, Ik'al and Votán, who were two sides of a coin—the same and yet opposites. When Ik'al turned out of sight, Votán would appear, and vice versa. But eventually Ik'al and Votán became stuck, immobilized, one fearing the night they faced, the other refusing to live in unending day.

Let's walk! one said suddenly. (They could never remember which.)

How? said Ik'al.

Where to? said Votán.

They realized that, simply by asking these two questions, they had in fact moved just a little.

Ever since, the gods walk with their questions and they never, ever stop.

"Questions, you see, are for walking," the Subcomandante concluded, "not just for standing still and doing nothing."

Anam Cara

BETH AND I DO NOT EAT POTATO CHIPS AND DRINK MARTINIS while discussing the merits of one method of suicide over another, as Anne Sexton did with Sylvia Plath.

We do not write each other long, impassioned letters like Ann Patchett and Lucy Grealy.

Neither is our friendship like that between Virginia Woolf and Katherine Mansfield: a broil of rivalries and jealousies plastered over with notes claiming undying inspiration and love.

Aristotle called friendship the art of holding up a mirror to each other's souls. That comes close to what I feel Beth and I are to each other. Emerson didn't try to come up with a definition of this abiding relationship, but he did extol its twin pillars of truth and tenderness, words that ring true to me.

All these attempts at defining the undefinable have a rightness to them, but when I think of my friendship with Beth, my mind settles on the Irish poet and philosopher John O'Donohue, who titled his masterwork *Anam Cara*, Gaelic for "soul-friend."

Originally, teachers and priests in the old Celtic religion were addressed as *anam cara*, people to whom you opened your mind and your heart. "This friendship," writes O'Donohue, "was an act of recognition and belonging. When you had an *anam cara*, your friendship cut across all convention, morality, and category. You were joined in an ancient and eternal way with the 'friend of your soul.' This art of belonging awakened and fostered a deep and special companionship."

My friendship with Beth cuts across age, across circumstance. Across everything.

Social acquaintance for me is too often greased with half-truths and posturing, as if we are each trying to recreate ourselves before the other. But within a true friendship, with an *anam cara*, I can be exactly who I am. Such openness, such lack of pretension, such vulnerability between friends is rare—it's a kind of love that makes life seem simple. As James Baldwin said of his great friend Toni Morrison: "I dig Toni, and I trust her."

Beth and I have this kind of relationship. We approach each other with integrity and honesty. When she doesn't like a piece in this book, she tells me and we work it out, adding and subtracting until it sits right with us both—or we get rid of it. I don't think there is anything we haven't talked about except perhaps money and sex. When we come up against boundaries, we respect them.

Friends, we agree, are like threads weaving through the tapestry of our lives. Some show up early and leave after a short time; others weave in and out over decades. Still others emerge only near the end. Each friend is unique, but they all share one quality: They are people who, as Jorge Luis Borges put it, "make us happy for the simple chance encounter of having crossed our path."

I feel understood in Beth's presence in a full and precious way. I hope she feels the same. We share truths with each other; we revel in our shared delights. We laugh. Inevitably, I walk away from our visits feeling refreshed, as if her friendship is an elixir I have sipped, an elixir that has changed me in the best possible way.

Inside this friendship, we are not seventy-three or a hundred and three. We are ageless. "The passionate heart never ages," writes O'Donohue, and that feels true too.

We are not the same. Each of us moves through life in our own way. Beth makes her collages with coloured thread and stamps and stones; she gathers circles of friends around her teapot. She looks for happiness and finds it. I tend my gardens, tilt my face to the birds, search for meaning in words. I look for happiness and I find it.

"I'm so glad," Beth says to me on our last phone call before another year ends. "I'm so very glad we are on this journey together."

Getting It Right

"PARTS OF ME ARE HUGELY EXCITED!" BETH EXCLAIMS WHEN I call the first week of January. A new year, a time for wishes and aspirations.

We have an excellent phone line today. I hear her as if she is in the room with me, in this pool of Mexican sunlight. She is sitting in her own pool of light, emanating from the full-spectrum daylight bulbs I sent to her a few weeks ago, when the days of the dying year were growing impossibly short and grey. Outside her window, freezing rain is building crystal sarcophagi around tree limbs. She has closed the drapes.

She is bursting to tell me about Tuesday, when two men came to collect the last of her enormous glass collection.

"It was my mother's pride and joy. When you came to dinner at her house, you sat down to a table of sparkling Canadian glass—plates, platters, pitchers, goblets, compote dishes of every size. As she was dying, she decided I would continue as the proselytizer of Canadian glass. For years Jack—what a hero!—lugged boxes of glass all over the province wherever I was invited to speak."

Beth's kitchen table was chockablock with glass when the two men arrived, carrying an offering of scones and a chocolate cake. "A treat for me. But I had to tell them I can't really eat sugar anymore."

She offered them tea. "'We don't drink tea,' they said. I asked them what they drink, and they said, 'We drink coffee.' The first time in my life someone refused my tea!"

Then she remembered the coffee her son Brian had left in her freezer when he moved out a few years before, a small bag with a spoonful or two in the bottom. "My coffee maker hadn't been out of the cupboard for seven years, but I still had some filter papers, so I dusted off the machine and poured in the coffee while the men packed up the glass. The whole time the liquid was bubbling through the coffee pot, I was thinking, *This could be absolutely putrid!*"

When the coffee was done and the glass was packed, she set the sweet treats on the table with plates and forks and serviettes—Beth always sets a proper table—and poured the coffee into mugs.

"'Okay, drink,' I said. Then, 'How is it?'" Beth is chortling. "'Perfect!!' they said. Can you believe it?"

We are both laughing like schoolgirls.

"And did they eat the cake?" I ask.

"They ate the whole damn thing!"

Beth is holding the list of questions I sent her, details I want to clarify for this project that has indeed become a book. We talk for a bit about dancing with Bettina Byers and travelling to Juno Beach with her daughter Gillian and her dancer pals David and Michael on the seventieth anniversary of D-Day, the Allied invasion of German-occupied France.

"It was important for me to go to Juno Beach. To mourn the patients I worked with," Beth explains.

I'm trying to tease out a timeline for her trips to Europe that in conversation have become conflated. It was the year before Juno

Beach that Beth and Gillian travelled to Italy. Seeing the countryside where Jim had spent the war moved her so deeply that when she returned home, she took out his letters, now yellowed and brittle with age, and created *Please Write*.

But she's telling me another story now, of an afternoon when she was standing with her daughter by a stone wall somewhere in Florence. Gillian has the map and they are trying to figure out how to get back to a shop where Beth spotted a black leather jacket she has decided she must have.

"An older man came along and said, 'I think if you turn the map around, you might find where you want to go.'"

We can't seem to stop laughing. Everything today strikes us as funny.

"That's excellent life advice!" I say when we catch our breath.

"Oh yes! How often we need to turn things around in order to see a way through."

The conversation veers to Paul, who died recently. Paul was my neighbour for fifteen years, but he was Beth's friend for seventy years. They celebrated birthdays together for decades, and after every visit to Oak Leaf Cottage he'd hand her a fragrant rose from his garden.

I show Beth the photograph Paul emailed to me when we were conferring on the details of the stone garden. In it, Beth is wearing a deep blue jumpsuit, her hand on her red, floppy-brimmed hat as she passes through the garden gate, striding into the middle distance.

"I haven't been able to find his obituary online," I say.

"Oh, I can solve that puzzle," Beth says. "Paul wrote his own obituary! David just sent it around to the newspapers."

I tell Beth about my friend whose mother also wrote her own obituary—over and over and over. It was a family pastime: Every year, the lot of them would haul out their obituaries and revise them with new triumphs, some real, some imagined.

"We should do that!" Beth exclaims.

"You start."

"Mine will be very short: 'In order to live and love as many years as I have, you must have passion—many passions!—exercise every day, and be nutritionally aware.'"

"And laughter," I say. "We can't forget that." I'm thinking of all the funny movies and stories and my husband's constant puns and cartoons that got me through the illness that has now left me, I hope for good.

"Oh yes," Beth says. "I do love to laugh."

We've been talking and laughing for an hour, relaxed in our pools of light, telling stories. Most of them I haven't heard before, even though we've been telling each other stories every week for three years.

I don't want to say goodbye, but I know I have to.

This Is Not the End

BETH AND I ARE WALKING BY THE LAKE. A SLOPE OF ROCKS separates the path from the water that lifts against them. Not quite waves: a soft, persistent lap. It is a colouring-book day, the air so clear that each leaf and twig seems outlined, the hues and tones filled in.

I think of the slogan I once saw stencilled on a restaurant tabletop: *Life is about using the whole box of crayons*. Nature does it without thinking.

Suddenly, Beth collapses against me. I stumble back, thrust my arm behind me, flailing until my fingers touch bark. I slide down the tree trunk, feeling for the ground, Beth awkwardly cradled against my chest.

"I'm dying," she says. A flat statement of fact.

The breeze is too soft, the sun too calmly warming for panic. "What do you want me to do?"

She shifts her hand over mine, presses it slightly. A pat that says, *Stay*.

I hitch myself more firmly against the tree and gently pull her rainbow scarf out from where it is balled between us. I smooth it over her shoulders, across her chest.

I kiss her hair.

I kiss her cheek.

I caress her arm, my other hand still under hers.

Beth looks up through the leaves, thin on the branches. I follow her gaze. The sky is a heartbreaking blue.

Her breaths come so softly I can't tell when they stop.

I imagine it like this, but the end could come in a hundred different ways. A bus T-boning her little Yaris. A fall in the bathtub, on her front steps, on some icy patch in the parking lot outside Food Basics. Covid. Pneumonia. Cancer. A burst vessel in the brain. A blocked artery in the lungs. An arrest of the heart.

It could as easily be my end as hers.

I could bear losing her like this, on the soft carpet of grass, leaves drifting down on us, the blue sky going on forever, waves lapping at stone, the air growing chill around us as our bodies lean into each other.

But I can't bear the thought of her leaving while I am here and she is there, so many thousands of miles between us.

Not now.

Not yet.

Acknowledgements

I WISH THANK-YOUS WERE FLOWERS SO I COULD HEAP THEM around Beth, without whom this book would not exist. I am grateful for her enthusiasm, her sharp intelligence, her openness, and her trust. "I have never not trusted you," she said as we wrapped up the last corrections, and that means more to me than I can say.

May I join your Grateful Society, Beth?

Friends have helped in so many ways: Leah Feldon, the brilliant photographer and landlady who rented us the house on the hill, where I turned a stack of notebooks into this book in a sun-bathed room overlooking the town where the bells of five cathedrals toll the hours of the day; Genni Gunn and Diane Schoemperlen, who interrupted their writing lives to read the manuscript; and what would I do without the friends who listened as I talked through this book, especially Jennifer Clement, Cathy Cooper, Pam Cross, Sandra Gulland, Gundi Harris, Chris Hixson, Jill Irwin, and Joan Jenner. I appreciate you all.

I feel privileged to work with Anne Collins, my editor at Random House Canada. Anne was my editor decades ago at *Saturday Night* magazine when it published my first short story; in the meantime she has climbed to the pinnacle of Canadian publishing, never for a moment losing her astonishing radar for the true heart of a story.

My agent, Marilyn Biderman, has been committed to this book from the beginning. The same is true of the Random House Canada team—especially the publisher, Sue Kuruvilla, and the managing editor, Deirdre Molina, who were among the first to read the manuscript, along with Polly Beel in marketing and Evan Klein in sales. What writer could ask for more?

A book is an idea made manifest. The ideas and words are mine (and Beth's), but the making-manifest part relies on the extraordinary skills of others. I feel privileged to have John Sweet as my copy editor, a skilled and seasoned catcher of gaffes and obfuscations. A special thank-you for those serial commas! My gratitude to the designer, Dylan Browne, and to Penguin Random House Canada's creative director Terri Nimmo, for making the book look beautiful on the page, and to publicity manager Shona Cook for getting the word out.

These past few years have been a challenge medically, one that continued through emergency surgery and a spinal fracture in Mexico as I prepared this book for publication. I am forever indebted to the friends who gathered around, bringing food and laughter, books and skin cream as I lay for months on my back—especially Jim McKeever and Alfredo Gracía-Lucio of Camino Silvestre, who provided a tranquil place where I recuperated amid hummingbirds, peacocks, and newborn chicks. My family of sisters and children and grandchildren are a constant joy and support; among them, the pillar in my life is my husband, Wayne Grady. I have always admired his fertile mind, his literary brilliance, and his hilarious cartoons, but in the past few years I have also been the grateful recipient of his endless kindness, his patience and forbearance, and his boundless capacity for love. Survival would be unthinkable without him.

MERILYN SIMONDS is the author of twenty books, most recently *Woman, Watching: Louise de Kiriline Lawrence and the Songbirds of Pimisi Bay*, an innovative memoir/biography of Lawrence, an extraordinary self-trained ornithologist who became one of Canada's greatest naturalists. Born in Winnipeg, Simonds grew up in small-town Ontario and Brazil. She published her first book in 1979 at the age of twenty-nine, and since then her work has been anthologized and published internationally in eight countries. She writes in a wide variety of genres—personal essay, memoir, travel, literary fiction (such as the novel *The Holding*, a *New York Times Book Review* Editors' Choice), and creative nonfiction, including *The Convict Lover*, which was a finalist for the Governor General's Literary Award for Non-fiction. In 2017, Project Bookmark Canada installed a plaque on the site of the former Kingston Penitentiary rock quarry to honour the place of *The Convict Lover* in Canada's literary landscape.